Dear Friend,

You are an explorer at the frontier to cyberspace at the dawning of a new era. Like the pioneers and settlers of times past, you may be somewhat apprehensive about the journey before you, uncertain of your destination, or of the challenges and perils before you. While much of what lies ahead is unknown, there are guides to help you along your path, but you will be creating maps of your own as you discover new territory.

Most importantly, you have the spirit and dedication needed to make this journey — a journey that will lead you to new vistas you will want to share with others.

I wish you the very best on your adventures. May they be filled with delight, and may your enthusiasm infect all those around you as they join in the transformation of education for the next century.

Warmest regards,

David Thornburg

3

Education in the Communication Age

*Give a student access to
the Internet and a place to
plug a modem, and she can
move worlds.*

(Archimedes updated)

David D. Thornburg, Ph.D.
DThornburg@aol.com

Thornburg, David D.
Education in the Communication Age

ISBN 0-942207-11-4 (pbk. plus CD-ROM)
Copyright © 1993, 1994 by David D. Thornburg and Starsong
Publications

Published in the United States of America.

ISBN 0-942207-11-4

Dr. Thornburg can be contacted at:
Thornburg Center
P. O. Box 7168
San Carlos, CA 94070

Contents

Foreword

The theme of this book, education in the Communication Age, is important. It is important because ongoing advances in technology are helping to shape a new world — a world in which lifelong learning is a survival skill, a world in which those who develop the skills to become self-directed learners will be far more successful than those who don't. It is a world punctuated by rapid change — a world for which the educational systems of our youth are ill-equipped to meet the needs of those who will lead us into the 21st century.

Twenty-five years ago, we set foot on the moon. To those of us who remember watching that event on television, the advances of the last quarter-century seem amazing. To our children, however, these advances are merely part of the fabric of their lives. Informational power tools like personal computers are a natural part of our children's world, even if they have not become commonplace in our classrooms.

As a nation, we have excelled in the development of the finest technologies in the world, yet many of these technologies have failed to penetrate our classrooms as thoroughly as they might. And, all too often, the few computers we do have in our classrooms are used to replicate the curriculum of the past, rather than to help prepare students for their future.

Against this backdrop we stand facing the dawn of a new era — the Communication Age. This era builds on the advances of the Information Age that preceded it, and promises to change the face of education in profound ways.

Washington has taken a leadership role in welcoming this new era through its active support of a National Information Infrastructure. This "informational superhighway" will only be meaningful to education if its benefits are brought to every learner and every educator in the country. This is why, on January 11, 1994, the Vice President said that we will connect all of our classrooms, all of our libraries, and all of our hospitals and clinics to the NII by the year 2000.

Universal access is so important that the President reiterated the Vice President's call to action during his 1994 State of the Union address.

The technological reality in today's classrooms is tragic. The head of the FCC, Reed Hundt, has said, "There are thousands of buildings in this country with millions of people in them who have no telephones, no cable television and no reasonable prospect of broadband services. They're called schools."

When it comes to ensuring universal service, our schools are the most impoverished institution in society. Only 14% of our public schools used educational networks in even one classroom last year. Only 22% possess even one modem. Only 4% even have phone lines in classrooms. If we allow the information superhighway to bypass education — even for an interim period — we will find that the information rich will get richer while the information poor get poorer with no guarantee that everyone will be on the network at some future date.

There are some fortunate students who are experiencing the future today. These students have high-speed access to the Internet and are able to collaborate on projects with their peers all over the world. Last year, for example, students in Germany and the United States collaborated on the design of aircraft using powerful simulation software and high-bandwidth communication lines that allowed them to share designs, to see, and to talk with each other, all through their personal computer systems. International boundaries evaporated as students were able to form friendships and work with their colleagues thousands of miles away.

This capability is just one example of the benefits awaiting learners in the Communication Age.

Yet, as explored in the pages that follow, the challenge is not just the new technology. It is holding true to our basic principles. The Vice President has said that whether our tools were the quill pens that wrote and then signed the Declaration of Independence or the laptop computers being used to write the constitutions of newly-freed countries, better communication has almost always led to greater freedom and greater economic growth.

That is our challenge. And that is the promise of education in the Communication Age.

Preface

This book is based on the premise that we are at the dawn of a new era — a time in history marked by rapid changes in all aspects of our lives. Virtually no segment of our economy will go untouched in the years to come. The transformation ahead of us will affect work, recreation, and education. It will impact young and old alike. It will, if we make the right choices, empower all people in our society to become constructive participants in our national dream. It can, if ignored, precipitate a widening of the gap between rich and poor.

I call the era we are entering the Communication Age. Like other ages that preceded it, this one builds on the advances society has already created; but, rather than move us further along a well-worn path, the transition from the Information Age to the Communication Age creates new paths for us to travel.

For many years I have devoted myself to thinking about education. My particular interest has been to think about how our educational system needs to transform itself to meet the needs of today's learners. As I have said before, our challenge is to prepare learners for their future, not for our past.

This book and accompanying CD-ROM attempt to address this challenge in the context of the Communication Age. Many of the ideas and resources shared in these pages (or on your computer) have always made sense, and probably always will. Others are especially relevant in a world that can be navigated by anyone with a personal computer and a modem connected to any phone line in the country.

I have several goals in this book: First, I want to set the stage for our entry to this new era. Second, I want to connect these ideas with our current national educational initiatives (such as the Goals 2000: Educate America Act of 1994.) Third, I want to provide practical information (and software tools) that will allow educators and their students to become cybernauts on the information highway. Finally, I want to provide (through a very cloudy crystal ball) some emergent ideas that may lead us to new ways of thinking about education in the coming years.

A Cautionary Note:

Words on paper (or CD-ROM) are frozen in time. Given the rapidity of change, it is virtually guaranteed that some of the ideas in this book will be out of date by the time you read them. The details, though, are less important than the overall vision. I beg your forgiveness for any errors that emerge, and hope that you find the overall ideas to be of value.

A Note on the CD-ROM:

Bound into the back of this book is a CD-ROM for the Macintosh series of computers. The decision to provide Macintosh-based software was driven by my familiarity with the computer, and the incredibly creative software that has been created for this platform by authors who have chosen to make their materials available as freeware or shareware.

This doesn't mean that the book is Macintosh-specific, only that the examples are (largely) illustrated with Macintosh versions of software that (in many cases) are starting to show up on other computers as well.

In browsing through the software on the CD-ROM, pay particular attention to the shareware notices. If you use any program for which the author has requested a fee, please pay it. The best way to insure the continued existence of excellent software at reasonable prices is to pay your fair share. In some cases, all the author wants is a postcard. In others, just a few dollars. Since the collection on this CD-ROM would cost thousands of dollars if full commercial versions of these software packages were included, any fee you are asked to pay is a bargain!

When I started this book, I was going to publish it completely on disc using the shareware multimedia authoring tool, DOCMaker. (I did include two chapters as DOCMaker documents.) I went back and forth on this decision, and finally decided to sacrifice a few more trees by publishing a printed version with all the software distributed on the CD-ROM.

Printed books are different from interactive media. We snuggle up with a good book. We do not (at this time) snuggle up with a good computer. Media are not inter-convertible, nor do new media obsolete the old. New media do transform old media, however, and this book and CD-ROM are an attempt to mark a transition along the path from one medium to the next.

I like to think of our technological tools as creating for us a magic carpet of the mind — a magic carpet with which we can explore the infinite world of ideas at the speed of thought. I hope your carpet ride is enjoyable, exciting, challenging, and invigorating. If it is, we will have succeeded in modeling the kinds of experiences that nurture the lifelong love of learning that forms the foundation of our future.

Acknowledgments

The ideas expressed in this book grew out of discussions with many people, and have been refined by participants in my presentations and workshops. While I can't list everyone who has helped me refine my thinking, I want to acknowledge several of my friends who have spent hours in conversation on the topics covered in this book: Ron Voth, Prasad Kaipa, Ed Fitzsimmons, Lynell Burmark, Sara Armstrong, Bernajean Porter, my wonderful wife, Pamela, and many many more. All my dear friends — both listed and unlisted — have enriched my life and are in my debt.

I take credit for any errors that may appear in this book.

DT • Monterey, California • August 1994.

Welcome to the Communication Age

It's not the content, it's the communication.

— *Jane Metcalf, Wired*

Have you had a hard time adjusting to the Information Age? If you're an educator, have you just not quite come up to speed on all the ways to use multimedia-based computers to enhance learning in your classrooms? If you're a parent, business person, or other community member interested in the improvement of education for all learners, have you been overwhelmed by all the fancy new computerized gadgets that promise to bring the merits of the Information Age into offices, classrooms and libraries in your community?

If so, take a deep breath and let out a sigh of relief. I have comforting news for you. You don't have to worry about the Information Age any more — it's all over.

Yes, that's right, the Information Age is over, dead, kaput, finito, nada, history, finished.

What killed it? And, more importantly, what is taking its place? More on that in a bit. For now, let's look at some evidence.

In the beginning of 1993, IBM announced that their losses had taken a sharp turn for the worse, even though the company did away with about 40,000 positions in 1992 — roughly double the 20,000 it had said would be cut. When the dust settled, IBM posted an annual loss of $6.865 billion, followed by an $8 billion, or $14.10 per share, loss in the second quarter of 1993. Continued cutbacks in staff and facilities stemmed the bleeding, but the patient was wounded. IBM, the company that virtually defined the information age, was reeling.

The cause for this was not that IBM was doing a bad job. Anyone who knows the company knows the high quality of their products and staff. No, the problem was not that IBM was doing a bad job; it was doing the wrong job.

IBM's loss was just one of the canaries in the coal mine; but, unlike those poor canaries that died in the presence of an odorless poison gas, IBM is not dead. In fact, it is rebounding. IBM Chairman Louis Gerstner announced in early 1994 that IBM is reducing its emphasis on mainframes and is going to get into the (Are you ready for this?) communication business. IBM got the message: adapt or die.

In our time of rapid change, (and things are moving so quickly that the very nature of change itself is changing,) a paradigm shift is sweeping the planet, leaving in its wake the carcasses of the lethargic dinosaurs that just didn't make the transition.

All of this is terribly important for schools, because the paradigm shift I am about to describe treats all institutions the same way. Businesses are at risk; our schools are at risk; our children are at risk. Education is no longer immune to the changes that are sweeping the planet at the speed of light.

To get a sense of what is going on, let's look at some of the major paradigm shifts of history.

The Birth of a New Age
George Gilder, author of *Life After Television* and other books on the future of technology, has a perspective that may shed some light on the emergence of ages. New ages come into existence when a new tool or technique produces a thousand-fold or more increase in efficiency.

For example, it can be argued that the domestication of animals and advances in farming produced incredible efficiencies over hunting and gathering. This transition paved the way for the Agricultural Age. Prior to the development of agriculture, people spent most of their lives in pursuit of food. Once agriculture took hold, surplus was created (leading to increased trade) and people could stay in one location and build cities.

Prior to the invention of the steam engine, energy was expensive unless you lived close to a river or waterfall. Animal or human-powered treadmills were highly inefficient sources of mechanical power. Animals needed food and rest. All this changed with the development of the steam engine. The steam engine made power virtually free, and paved the way for the Industrial Age.

In the early days of computers, information storage, switching and computing were quite expensive — many dollars per bit. Today's dense integrated circuits have reduced the cost of this hardware to under a thousandth of a cent per bit, thus setting the stage for the Information Age.

Compare your computer with the ENIAC (completed in 1946). It cost a fortune, weighed 30 tons and operated at one three-hundredth the speed of a typical personal computer today — with only a tiny fraction of your computer's memory!

To get some sense of how rapidly technology has advanced, think about this: Have you ever received one of those greeting cards that play music or the sender's voice message when you open it? If you throw one of those away, you'll be discarding more computing power than existed in the entire world prior to 1950.

The technological advances that created the Information Age have been phenomenal, and show no sign of letting up. Even so, we are at the brink of still another new era — the Communication Age.

Why? Because perceived bandwidth is becoming virtually free. Breakthroughs in the compression and transmission of data of all kinds promise to send information at blindingly fast data rates through strands of glass or through the freest medium of all — the space that surround us.

To get just a glimpse of what lies in store for us, sometime in 1995, the United States will demonstrate a network operating at a data transmission rate of 100 gigabits per second. This would allow the contents of 20 CD-ROMs to be transmitted in one second. Put another way, data transmission at this rate would allow the entire contents of a typical city library to be sent in less than 10 seconds. By the year 2000, it is possible that we will be measuring network speeds in "libraries per second". And, even at these phenomenal rates, we would still be operating 250 times slower than the intrinsic data-carrying capacity of glass fibers.

The Nature of Ages

Largely because of the writings of Alvin Toffler (*The Third Wave*) and other like-minded futurists, the notion of historical ages dating back to the creation of agriculture some 10,000 years ago has gained popularity. One common misperception resulting from this view of history is that each new age displaces the preceding age — that the Industrial Age displaced the Agricultural Age, for example.

Ages are a bit more complicated than that. New ages do not displace old ones, but they do transform them. For example, the Industrial Age provided many tools of benefit to Agriculture, and did much to improve the efficiency of farming. Many people don't realize that the first assembly line was NOT created by Henry Ford to build cars; it was built many years before by Eli Whitney, one of the great names in agricultural equipment. The later development of the mechanized reaper allowed even greater efficiencies in food production. Modern farming takes place on a scale unthinkable prior to the Industrial Age.

By the same token, industry made widespread use of the tools of the Information Age to improve the productivity of factories. Further advances in computer use in industry expanded to include computer-assisted design and drafting, inventory

16

control, and robotics, to name just a few. The flattening of hierarchies in organizational structures was enabled by the ability of workers at all levels of an organization to have immediate access to in-depth information on their business. In addition to making corporations more efficient, it shortened the decision cycle time, allowing corporations to be more responsive to customer needs.

One modern consequence of the transformations industry has experienced as a result of the Information Age has been the development of the "virtual corporation" in which production takes place closer and closer to the customer. Bar-coded items in stores not only simplify transactions, they provide a database that is then provided to manufacturers to help them plan new products. The feedback loop from customer to manufacturer has become so tight today, that niche products can be conceived, moved into manufacturing, and sold to consumers in a fraction of the time needed a generation ago.

And now that we have entered the Communication Age, we can expect this era to have its impact on our informational tools. Already we are seeing the remote distribution of software. Physical possession of VCR rental tapes and game cartridges, for example, will be replaced by versions of these products piped into our homes through cable or satellite downlinks. Already 60% of American homes have cable, and an additional 30% can be connected overnight. A new "digital broadcast satellite" (DBS) service will bring hundreds of channels to any home for $700 and a spare place to set a small receiving dish the size of a serving plate.

I expect similar transformations to take place with computer software as well. One advantage of electronic distribution is that upgrades are instantaneous, and vendors don't have to worry about a pipeline of product in inventory tying up corporate resources while waiting to be sold. Of course, rapid movement to this method of software distribution could mark the end of software retailing as we know it. Apple Computer, Inc. and other companies are already distributing free CD-ROM's filled with commercial software packages that can be

17

purchased by phoning in a credit card number in exchange for an unlocking code that provides access to the software on the disc.

Strip Malls on Disc

Computer software isn't the only commercial product available through CD-ROM distribution. Enterprising companies like The Merchant (1-800-561-3114) have placed interactive catalogs from numerous stores like Land's End, Brookstone, EarthBeat, and many more on a CD-ROM where users can browse at their leisure and accumulate orders that are then placed directly from the computer. Rather than manage a shopping center and incur the construction, insurance and maintenance costs associated with a physical site, The Merchant brings the shopping mall to your desktop where you can browse to your heart's content and place your order when you are ready to act. Your private interactive shopping mall is open 24-hours a day, 365 days a year, and shopkeepers of all sizes can take part.

While this type of shopping eliminates the social aspect of haunting the malls, it definitely provides interesting alternatives to shops that would otherwise have to outfit and staff storefronts. In comparison to physical stores, shelf space is free in cyberspace.

In the future, as high bandwidth pipes enter our homes and businesses, even the CD-ROM won't be needed. Software will be purchased directly over the Net, completely bypassing traditional retail channels. This will open new opportunities for those who choose to anticipate and master the trend. But those who ignore the advent of the Communication Age may find themselves reduced from selling Apple Macintoshes in a computer store to selling McIntosh apples on the street corner.

The Communication Age will impact our informational tools in other ways as well. Just as software will become "softwhere", our traditional informational resources (encyclopedias, reference works, etc.) will also reside on the Net. In fact, they are already there. The problem today is that the pipeline is too skinny to get this information at the data rates we might like. All of this is changing, and changing fast. There is little question that the Communication Age will send out ripples that will change the face of information, industry and agriculture.

Education's New Challenge

The rapid arrival of this new era is catching everyone by surprise, and, for once, the private sector is grappling with the issue at the same time as education. Some well-established corporate institutions are falling apart or struggling to survive, and business plans are being frantically rewritten in order to secure some kind of future for companies whose present productivity is based on an outmoded paradigm.

For example, it doesn't take much of a crystal ball to realize that Blockbuster Video will soon be offering completely different services — or will simply cease to exist. This has nothing whatever to do with the quality of their existing service, or the excellence of their workers; it has simply to do with the fact that their current business — software rental — will be rendered obsolete when bandwidth becomes free and Blockbuster's current product line gets piped directly into homes over the Net. (Fortunately, Blockbuster understands this and is already positioning itself for the Communication Age by offering products that take advantage of telecommunications.)

This is an important point. In the traditional free market economy, companies competed on service and quality within a fixed product domain. Blockbuster competed with Wherehouse in video rentals, for example. Now the rules of the game have completely changed, and mastery in the old game has become meaningless. Blockbuster is competing with the phone companies and cable television operators — entities that wouldn't show up on a traditional list of competitors in software rental. This means that companies like AT&T will soon be competing with Blockbuster!

AT&T announced a modem for Sega Genesis video games called "The Edge" early in 1993. With this attachment, two game players could connect with each other over the telephone for the purpose of playing games. AT&T pretty much had the concept to themselves until mid-1994 when Blockbuster Entertainment and Davis Video combined forces to create Catapault Entertainment, a new company that will also sell modems designed to link video game players over ordinary telephone lines. These modems will be sold as add-ons for the many millions of Sega Genesis and Super Nintendo game systems found in our homes. The Blockbuster service operates over a gaming network to connect players with each other, as well as to provide gaming tips and other relevant information.

Applied to education, the message is similarly clear: The quality of our current schools, curriculum, staff, and resources is not the issue. The issue, quite simply, is how we transform education to meet the needs of today's students. Make no mistake, education will change whether we drive that change or not. In that area, education is in the same boat as Blockbuster Video. Unless we quickly move to take proactive control of the change process, our educational institutions may become irrelevant to the education of our youth. If that happens, they will simply disappear.

Historically, we've had it fairly easy. Our educational institutions, in general, met the needs of the agrarian and industrial economies, reflecting a period when people learned enough in school to secure a job in one field that they would keep until retirement. Job transitions were typically made within one industry, and on-the-job training generally paved the way for advancement. Today's world, involving five or six career changes in a lifetime, is quite a different place.

Numerous reports such as the SCANS materials from the United States Department of Labor, the Magaziner report, *America's Choice: High Skills or Low Wages*, and Robert Reich's *Work of Nations* all point to the same challenge: People who are flexible, lifelong learners with a tolerance for ambiguity and a sense of self-direction can develop the high skills needed to secure high-paying jobs that build our economy. Those who lack these skills are locked into low paying jobs or, worse yet, no jobs at all.

As Labor Secretary Reich states, when our current economic recovery is examined, our citizens are on one of two staircases: one leading up, and another leading down. The only people on the "up" staircase are those with high skills.

If you doubt this, look at the graph below compiled from U. S. Census Bureau data.

% Income Change, U.S. Males, 1969-1989

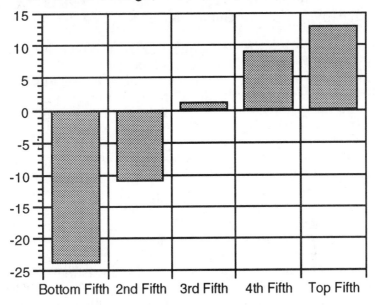

Workers at the lowest end of the wage (and skill) spectrum have seen their incomes decline by about 25% in the two decades from 1969 to 1989. Furthermore, many of the low paying jobs are disappearing altogether, never to return. The situation for women in this same time period differs in that women's wages rose in all categories, although the gap between low and high wages increased by about the same amount as that for men.

Highly skilled workers, on the other hand, are seeing their incomes rise. While it is true that even highly skilled workers are finding jobs in large corporations to be quite unstable, their skill base insures that they can find employment elsewhere or, increasingly, start new ventures on their own. An educational system that addresses the reality implicit in this graph is quite different from the one that met the needs of past generations of students.

Doing Different Things vs. Doing Things Differently...

Historically, technological innovations of the Information Age moved into classrooms slowly, and many of these tools were used to perpetuate a curriculum wedded to the past.

In visiting computer labs across the country, I've seen students with access to lots of technology, but armed with this information alone I can't tell if the technology is being used to replicate workbooks, or to develop the kinds of skills and practices needed to thrive in the future. The presence of technology by itself is no indicator of its effective use.

The grace period is over. No longer can we allow outdated institutions to proceed at a snail's pace into a future zooming ahead at the speed of light — the gap is already stretched to the limit, and the thread connecting many current schools to society's needs is about to break. This has profound implications for technology use in education. Any attempt to think of these tools as "productivity enhancers" will fail if we use them to enhance the productivity of the existing system. What merit is there in increasing the efficiency with which we can pump even more students into the world without the kinds of skills and attitudes they need to thrive in the coming years?

Fortunately, the technology of the Communication Age dovetails with the needs of America's students. Every competency and skill described in any of the documents referenced above fits naturally in an educational setting in which technology is used to help self-directed learners acquire and model the skills they need.

Communication Age Needs for Education

In order for technology to have the impact it should on education, there are four key issues to be addressed. Building on the popularity of the information highway (or, more recently, the "infobahn"), *every* learner and educator must have:

- **Equitable access to on-ramps:**
  (anywhere, any time access to the Net)

- **Interesting destinations:**
  (worthwhile places to explore, e.g., all the great museums, libraries, and research centers of the world)

- **Access to vehicles:**
  (universal access to the computers needed to traverse the infobahn at home, at school, and in libraries)

- **Driver's education:**
  (understanding of how the tools of the Communication Age can be used to build the future, not replicate the past and the skills to incorporate modern technologies into a reinvented curriculum in which learning is self-directed and lifelong)

Changes

The very nature of change itself is changing. Any long-term plan that does not allow for radical modification is doomed to failure. We need to shorten the time frame for bringing the benefit of innovations to all students, whether these innovations arise from the domains of pedagogy, curriculum, or technology.

For example, even though the utility of telephones has been proven since 1876, most classrooms in our country lack this simple technology. This abomination must be rectified immediately. Informational highways are meaningless to those who lack access to on-ramps. And yet one can see why telephones have not spread into classrooms. First, they are expensive. Second, their use is hard to monitor and project. The first issue can be rectified by having the Public Utilities Commission in each region of our country produce a new tariff for schools — a tariff that makes phone lines affordable for schools, yet guarantees long term profitability to the service provider.

Once phone lines are installed, the classroom must have adequate technology to allow these phone lines to act as informational gateways for our young people. In the next chapter we show that powerful technology can be provided for every student and educator for a mere 2% of our educational budget. We need to invest only two pennies of our educational dollar to provide access to powerful technology to EVERY learner and educator.

The mere existence of technology does nothing to insure its effective use, however. Staff development and participation in the reinvention of our educational system is essential for long-term success. A portion of the two cents mentioned above would provide enough money for ongoing staff development. More importantly, educators need to see themselves as full-time professionals — paid to work year-round (with a few weeks for vacation). Students might be present for 180 or so of those days, but the rest of the time educators would be reinventing themselves. This shift in mindset presents a far greater challenge than finding the money to pay for it.

Working & Learning in the Communication Age

While I am painfully aware that those who live by the crystal ball shall eat crushed glass, I can't resist sharing perspectives on the emergent trends of the Communication Age and speculating on their potential impact on education. If there is an underlying message that permeates these trends, and retains validity even if we are mistaken in the details, it is this: Our challenge is not to do old things differently, it is to do different things. In the past, technological innovations in education have either been put on a shelf and forgotten, or they have been used to make small adjustments to the existing curriculum. Yes, some innovative schools have created radical transformations, but these noble steps have yet to foment revolution in education at large.

Our task is clear: As frightening as it may be, we need to completely revamp educational practice in light of societal transformations that have accumulated since the common schools in the 1830's. I am convinced that educators have the basic skills needed to create this transformation, and that they will apply their skills toward that end once we provide the support they need to do the job properly. The Communication Age has shrunk the world to pocket size — there is no place to hide. Short of time travel back to the 1950's, change-resistant people in both the public and private sector have no options: change is inevitable.

If we truly engage in the challenge of transforming education with the assistance of the technological tools we have invented, then we will have gone a long way toward building a future in which we can all thrive. Our challenge, quite simply, is to use our tools to prepare people for their future, not for our past.

The 2% Solution

If you think education is expensive, try ignorance!

— *Anonymous*

Universal, unlimited, anywhere, any time access to powerful telecomputers can help children of all ages retain their love for learning, improve academic performance, and help prepare them for a world in which self-directed lifelong learning is a survival skill. Indiana's Buddy System, for example, has shown the kind of results that accrue from kids having computers at home. Unlimited universal access to educational computing (with telecommunication links to other students and educators) has resulted in improved academic performance, improved enthusiasm for learning, and has even provided an effective lengthening of the school year by several days, just because of the extra time students spent on-line from home after school. (For more information, the Buddy System can be contacted at 317-231-7145.)

Unfortunately, pilot projects like the Buddy System reach only a few of our youth. The Buddy System currently operates in about fifty schools scattered throughout Indiana. Other ambitious projects, such as Apple's Classroom of Tomorrow (ACOT) are similarly small in scope. In the meantime, some children have access to powerful technology provided by their parents, while huge numbers of would-be learners because their families lack interest or financial resources.

If we accept the premise that universal access to powerful computational and telecommunications technology is an essential component of being a productive citizen in the Communication Age, then immediate steps must be taken to insure that economic differences do not create a bifurcated society of (informational) "haves" and "have-nots" in which those who cannot afford access to the power of telecomputing and other informational technologies are relegated to a permanent backwater of unemployability and non-productive lives.

Funding

One argument that has been used to rationalize our apparent unwillingness to equip every learner with technology is funding — or more precisely — the perceived lack of it. On the surface, the cost of equipping every student and educator with today's technology is staggering, especially given the increasingly tight constraints placed on state education budgets.

How would you feel if I showed you a funding plan that is tractable, would assist in America's economic growth, would provide powerful technology to every child, would insure that this technology is used in meaningful, productive ways to meet both the national goals and the needs of new workers, and would provide the critical mass of incentives to bring our educational system into alignment with the needs of the next century?

If this sounds too good to be true, read on!

The Equipment

Before describing the plan, we need first to suggest a basic computer configuration that would be of utility to learners and educators alike. Based on 1994 technology, the core system would have at least a 80 megabyte hard disk, a floppy drive, 8 megabytes of RAM, a built-in CD-ROM drive, a color display with a resolution of 640x480 pixels (8-bit image quality), a 14.4 kbaud modem, an ink-jet printer, and an integrated software package including word processor, spreadsheet, database, graphics and telecommunications programs. In addition, a multimedia authoring tool would be provided.

Cost and Financing

One plan we describe assumes that the technology listed above would be made available to each year's incoming class of third grade students. (The program could start earlier if desired.) The technology would be provided at the end of second grade so students could get used to the equipment before their next grade starts. In many states this would result in sales of about 50,000 systems each Fall. In California, this number would be closer to 400,000. The purchase price of the system just described, in quantities this large, would probably be in the range of $1,000. We add $300 to this number to provide technology and extensive staff development for teachers.

One proposal (Plan A below) is that the technology is introduced at one grade level, and that the computer equipment becomes the personal property of the student to use in perpetuity. Given the rate at which technology undergoes continued development, students will need an upgraded system and software after five years.

The State of California currently invests about $5,000 per student each year in grades K-12. We propose increasing this amount slightly to finance the acquisition of the computer technology described above. Since the increased expenditure would be spread among all 13 grades, this amounts to only $100 more per student per year, bringing the new investment in our youth to about $5,100 per year. This amounts to only a 2% increase in education spending per child for the first five years of the program. Once the first group of students enters the eighth grade the program cost may rise a bit when students get the upgraded equipment and software. On the other hand, the expenditures might not double then. High tech equipment continues to drop in price and improve in performance. Depending on the mix of features that are needed in an upgraded system, the incremental cost for the upgraded system might be offset by an overall reduction of prices for technology at all grade levels. For example, computer hardware prices are dropping at about 30% per year for fixed performance, and performance is doubling every two years. It is highly likely that more powerful systems will be available in five years for a fraction of their cost today. For example, I've been told that Nintendo's Reality Engine — a new $250 computer system that will be on the market in 1995 — outperforms the original Cray supercomputers that sold for several million dollars apiece.

The staff development and teacher equipment allowance works out to about $7,500 per teacher (assuming a student/teacher ratio of 25:1). $1,000 of this amount would be allocated to the teacher's computer system, with additional money invested in classroom technology (e.g., liquid-crystal display plate, laser videodisc player, video projection system, etc.), leaving several thousand dollars per teacher for professional development. The staff development would be ongoing, and would connect with current efforts to reinvent education, with a special emphasis on reinventing both the curriculum and instructional strategies, as well as on integrating technology into daily classroom practice.

Plan A

In the first year, all students entering third grade would receive their equipment during the break after second grade. All third-grade teachers would receive their equipment then and be provided with an extensive staff development program designed to help them reinvent their educational practice. The following year, the next group of new third-graders would receive their equipment, and the staff development focus would switch to the fourth grade, and so on. The equipment provided at each year would reflect advances in technology during the previous year. As the program continues, the quality of the technology improves and its cost declines.

At the end of seventh grade, students would upgrade their equipment and software to the current offering. New teachers teaching any grade level would, of course, receive the equipment being used at that level. New students entering any grade level for which technology has been introduced would receive the technology as part of their admission to the school unless they already had been provided with the technology at their previous school.

29

Plan B

Instead of introducing technology at one grade level at a time, the technology would be introduced at grades 3 and 8 simultaneously. Grade 8 would continue to be the grade at which equipment is upgraded for those who entered the program at the third grade. Staff development needs would double under this plan, as would the initial cost of implementation.

Networking and Service

In addition to the expenses mentioned above, there are additional expenses connected with network access from students' homes and the technical support required by students and teachers to keep their equipment in top condition.

Since some states already have statewide educational networks, I envision an expansion of this service to reach a much larger audience. States lacking such a system would need to create one anyway in order to participate in the National Information Infrastructure. These costs are separate, and are not reflected in my calculations.

Software and equipment maintenance is quite expensive. On the other hand, we currently have a large shift in workforce resulted from the downsizing of the military, and envision people being trained as computer technicians through school-to-work initiatives getting their practical experience by providing the services needed for educators and learners.

Challenges

- Most states would need to expand their educational network access greatly to accommodate the increased telecommunications traffic needed to support this plan. Furthermore, local high-speed access nodes at schools and districts would need to be established. These local nodes would then serve as gateways to the statewide and national information infrastructure.

- Sources of funding to increase the expenditure per learner would need to be found. Additional tax revenues must be generated, or the funds would need to be reallocated from the current educational budget. Because this plan represents a permanent change in educational funding, short-term grants are not appropriate sources of revenue.

- Technology use under this plan needs to take advantage of the discoveries and benefits found through the many wonderful model technology programs that have been established all over the country in the last few years. Dissemination and integration of the best parts of these programs need to be funded as well.

- The staff development needs, funded by 30% of the money allocated to this plan, will severely tax the in-service programs currently in place. We must insure that new staff development programs are created that meet the needs of reinvented schools, and that these programs are brought to every teacher in a timely fashion in a manner that insures ongoing support for systemic change. The role of technology as one of the staff development tools needs to be explored. Both telecommunications-based delivery and CD-ROM-based materials can supplement classroom based instruction for educators. The staff development program would implement the same strategies for learning that we wish educators to use with their own students.

- The long-term service of the equipment and software needs to be addressed. While short-term solutions may result from defense conversion funds, the cost of maintaining these systems must be anticipated.

- Strategies for the enticement of grade-specific educational software development need to be explored. States could fund software development in exchange for lifetime royalty-free license to the software. The developers would be free to sell their product out of their state, should they choose to do so.

Benefits

This plan has numerous benefits far outweighing its modest cost:

- Every child will have equitable access to powerful technology, independent of social or economic status.

- By transforming the informational tools available to every child at once, the transformation of educational strategies will be automatic — no longer can it be argued that outdated instructional methodologies be retained because the new tools are restricted to only a small percentage of our youth.

- Universal access to technology permits easy introduction of the new curricular frameworks, since all educators at each grade level will be involved in an intensive staff development effort anyway.

- By introducing the technology at one or two grade levels at a time, the major staff development effort will be easier to implement than if it were brought to all grades simultaneously.

- The infusion of technology into the homes of teachers and students alike provides a much needed shot in the arm for the vendors of this equipment, and special consideration could be given to local companies.

- The presence of these computers will incentivize the creation of high quality educational software, since a ready market will exist.

- Ancillary sales of software and peripherals through traditional retail channels will help boost local economies.

We hear much about the need to transform education in our country, and while unlimited access to technology is not a solution in itself, it does represent a powerful vehicle and context in which broader transformations can take place.

Shifting the Vision

Francis Bacon, 1561-1626   Thomas Jefferson, 1743-1826

Dear Mr. Jefferson,

I am in receipt (through the miracle of Time Travel) of some of your missives re: the desirability of an educated populace. I must say (from my vantage point of the 1600's) that your thoughts are noble but dangerous nonetheless.

Surely you don't truly believe that everyone should be educated!

Your most humble servant,

Francis Bacon
FBacon@rosicrucian.org

My Dear Francis,

Thank you for your message of Tuesday last. I, too, am in receipt of your writings, although I did not need such amazing technology as you seem to have at your disposal since it is now 1800 and your works are well known in our new country.

Yes, I do believe in the free and open access to information by everyone — it is the only foundation on which a self-regulated Democracy can be built, and on which our modest Republick can survive.

Most truly yours,

Thos. Jefferson
TJefferson@virginia.edu

Most honored colleague,

Might I beg to remind you, kind sir, that when I said "Knowledge is power," that I meant that most literally. He who has the knowledge wields the power. If this knowledge is shared indiscriminately, its power is lost. As I've said just this year (1601):

"Nothing destroys authority so much as the unequal and untimely interchange of power, pressed too far and relaxed too much."

Your experiment with Democracy is in its infancy. I think you might be still heady from the victory you extracted from my noble country (and don't think I have not forewarned Q. Eliz. of what disaster might befall this great nation some 175 years hence), but the notion of the free and open interchange of information is likely to make people unruly if they don't know how to use this information properly.

Better, I say, to grant the rudiments (words and ciphers, &c.) to those capable of grasping them, and keep the true learning for those who can appreciate its value. Look at the power that accrued as a result of the Crusades. All manner of knowledge relating to the math, sciences, art, and musick have been attained (at no small cost to either side!) by those in power where much of it is still kept safe from prying eyes and minds.

Your most humble and obedient servant,

Francis Bacon
FBacon@rosicrucian.org

Most ostentatious colleague,

Might I remind you that you, yourself, are highly educated, and that your own education did not diminish that of your teachers. I have been engaged in related (but more amicable) discourse on this very topic with Dr. Benj. Franklin (BFrankin@embassy.gov). He is of the opinion that ideas should be shared, with protection for the authors and creators of original works. You might be interested in my position:

"If nature has made any one thing less susceptible than all others of exclusive property, it is the action of the thinking power called an idea, which an individual may exclusively possess as long as he keeps it to himself; but the moment it is divulged, it forces itself into the possession of everyone, and the receiver cannot dispossess himself of it. Its peculiar character, too, is that no one possesses the less, because every other possesses the whole of it. He who receives an idea from me, receives instruction himself without lessening mine; as he who lights his taper at mine, receives light without darkening me.

"That ideas should freely spread from one to another over the globe, for the moral and mutual instruction of man, and improvement of his condition, seems to have been peculiarly and benevolently designed by nature, when she made them, like fire, expansible over all space, without lessening their density at any point, and like the air in which we breathe, move, and have our physical being, incapable of confinement or exclusive appropriation."

Most humbly yours,

Thos. Jefferson
TJefferson@whitehouse.gov

My Dear Yankee Twit,

Your ideas have brought tears of laughter to the members of my small society (one of whose future members is your esteemed Dr. Franklin.) Clearly we have differences of opinion.

History will be the judge of the correctness of our respective thoughts. Without belabouring the point, the ideas I express have stood the test of time since the Middle Ages. Yours are of such recent vintage that one cannot tell their quality at this time.

I would continue this dialogue, but the Queen has taken a fancy to a local playwright — a popular author of romances and tragedies — whose deathless prose is in obvious need of some assistance. I have agreed to help with one of his dreadful tragedies set in Denmark. Something about a prince — I'll obtain the gory details at dinner this evening, if I can stay awake.

Yours through time and space,

Francis Bacon
FBacon@rosicrucian.org

Bringing Home the Bacon

While Thomas Jefferson and Francis Bacon lived almost 200 years apart, they were both excellent thinkers devoted to exploring the power of ideas in the hands of the populace. The (obviously) fictitious chain of e-mail attempts to explore one of the areas where these two great thinkers might have disagreed. (Any text in the e-mail enclosed in quotation marks is directly taken from the writings of these authors.)

My reason for leading off this section with the thoughts of these two men is that they are related to a challenge facing education today as we strive to reinvent our institutions for the Communication Age.

Think about the teachers you had when you were in school. Many of them would feel quite at home with Francis Bacon. To these teachers, information was a scarce resource to be metered out in chunks to students who then memorized them as precious tidbits to be given back in the next examination. The structure of these teachers' classrooms was supportive of the idea that they who have the knowledge wield the power. Classroom technologies that supported this power base (e.g., blackboards and textbooks with teacher's editions) were embraced, and technologies that eroded this perspective (e.g., student computer use built around open-ended tools such as Logo) were rejected.

When the blackboard is in the front of the room, and all the seats are rows, and the teacher is towering over the students, the position of power is clearly established just by the structure of the environment. If you doubt this, imagine walking into a classroom filled with adults the same age as the teacher. Could you tell, just from the relative location of the people in the room who the teacher was? In almost all cases you could.

As for the book, this technology took quite a while to make it into classrooms. Prior to inexpensive printed books, teachers read their copies verbatim to students who then transcribed their own versions. Once mass-produced books appeared, educators resisted their encroachment into classrooms since this diluted the information-delivery power of the teacher. Fortunately, the inventor of the "teacher's edition" saved the day by insuring that the copy held by the teacher still had more information than copies in the hands of the students.

When personal computers starting showing up in schools in the late 1970's, many teachers were delighted to see equipment moved into labs where their use could be restricted and monitored. In many cases, the only software made available to students perpetuated the old curriculum.

Francis Bacon would have been proud, but none of us should be surprised. Our schools were modeled after those in Europe, and those grew out of the very group who, in the Middle Ages and later, maintained their hierarchical power structure through restricted access to knowledge.

If the classrooms of our youth were Baconian, libraries were (and are) Jeffersonian. Rather than operating on the notion that information is a scarce resource that must be carefully metered out to people, librarians know that information is an infinite resource that people need to learn how to access it when they need it. Librarians are, at their core, Jeffersonians of the first order.

What happens when all our classrooms and homes contain on-ramps to the infobahn? At that point, the underlying structure of school is turned on its head. Students with Net access experience the infinite quantity of information first hand (and are often overwhelmed by it). Baconian educators are threatened because the delivery of facts can now come in such depth and breadth that the metering of information is virtually impossible. The very structure of school as we knew it is threatened by this technology.

My guess is that this is one reason why schools are the only information-intensive system in our society in which telephone lines are not found on virtually every worker's desk. Even the teachers themselves are denied telephone access from their rooms. In more than one case I've been told (by principals)

41

that this is to insure that they spend their time teaching, not gabbing on the phone.

The "expense" of providing phone lines to classrooms is also used as an excuse for lack of access, yet it would cost no more to patch classrooms to the school's phone system than it would to patch them to the school's PA system. Wires are wires — they don't care what they carry. A school PA system maintains Baconian hierarchy, of course. The site administrator can interrupt any or all classes at any time, but teachers can only send messages to the main office.

Organizations Fight for Survival

Given education's capacity to resist technology in the past, won't schools simply ignore the information highway?

I don't think they can. The info-genie is out of the bottle. Some students (those from well-educated high-income households) already have Net access at home, and millions more will be added to this number in the coming years. One out of three American homes has a personal computer in it today, and that percentage is increasing. These computers are under $30 away from having a modem providing at least some minimal sort of Net access.

Students who can explore the vast resources available to them from the comfort of their home will become increasingly impatient with traditional classroom practice. Unless all educators come to understand that the technology of the Communication Age mandates a rapid move from a Baconian to a Jeffersonian paradigm, we risk having schools become irrelevant to the educational process.

Paradigm shifting is not easy, of course. While, in the new world, educators still have a lot of power, the nature of this power is quite different, and hence the transition is scary for many.

Education is not alone in its reluctance to shift views. Consider, for example, one of the fundamental differences between the cable television companies and the telephone companies. About 60% of all American homes have connections to both of these services. The TV cable has a bandwidth thousands of times greater than that of the telephone line, yet the cable operators are first class Baconians. They behave as if bandwidth is a scarce resource and feel comfortable dictating what will be shown. By decree, cable operators set up their tiers of programming and present viewers with a fixed menu of choices. This paternalistic attitude is accepted by the public because (I guess) we don't know any better. Once a cable company decides to drop one service in favor of another, our calls and letters of protest rarely have any influence.

The telephone companies, on the other hand, currently have very little bandwidth in our homes (compared with the cable operators), yet they are Jeffersonian in their use of the lines. The phone companies don't care where, when, or for how long you use their lines. All they care about is *that* you use them. Rather than dictate a palette of services from which you must choose, the telephone companies stress the ease with which you can dial virtually anywhere in the world 24-hours a day. Historically, this mode of operation may be an outgrowth of the fact that regulators have not allowed phone companies to be information providers, but the result is that cable operators and telephone companies operate from philosophically opposed camps. This philosophical rift may have contributed to some of the difficulties that emerged in 1993 as some of the cable/telco attempts at joint ventures fell apart.

Of course, as the phone companies increase their bandwidth, they will have even greater power to promote Jeffersonian ideals.

John Malone, President of TCI, the largest cable company in the United States, claims that he will build the country's information infrastructure for us by 1996. What he fails to mention is that this infrastructure is a lot more than glass and copper — it operates with an underlying philosophy. The philosophy he espouses is Baconian and antithetical to the kinds of open-ended free exploration of ideas that form the basis of the educational revolution now at hand. Malone and his colleagues are building a system that is still based on a closed set of services. Just because our choices have moved from 50 to 500, or our selection method has changed from the twist of a channel knob to the click of a mouse does not change the underlying model of the cable operator's paradigm.

This doesn't mean that the cable operators can't change their underlying philosophy. In the long term they will have to. In July, 1994, Time Warner received permission to provide telephone service over its cable television lines in New York City. As the cable companies continue their glassification of America, with fiber optic cables being laid at a prodigious rate, high-bandwidth two-way communication is virtually a free byproduct of this infrastructure upgrade. Any attempt to restrict the return path from homes, schools and businesses will be rejected by a nation who has experienced the Jeffersonian freedom of the telephone for over a century.

The coming years will be interesting to watch as the battles between the telephone companies and cable operators escalate. Amidst all the potential mergers and financial deals being initiated and broken lies a deeper philosophical battle, however. It is a battle we will all win if Jeffersonian ideals prevail.

Moving back into the classroom, I think I now understand why some teachers are happy to have cable in the classroom, but reluctant to have computers hooked up to modems. Most classrooms in the United States have at least some access to television and/or a VCR; but only 4% of the classrooms in our schools have modems in them.

The cable companies are comrades in arms of lecture-based teachers. They understand each other perfectly, just as the members of the Rosicrucians did when they shared their little secrets among themselves. ("Pity that Galileo couldn't keep his mouth shut. He's right, of course, but going public with ideas like his — imagine! We have to stop him, of course, before he gets out of hand.")

The transformation of education that is needed to take advantage of the Communication Age has little to do with the cost of the associated technology. It is, instead, a philosophical battle that will shake the underlying premise of our schools to their core: Are we in the business of teaching our youth, or of facilitating their learning? It is this question that marks the dividing line between the outmoded world of Bacon and the Jeffersonian ideals needed to prepare us all for life in the next century.

What Are We to Do?

Luckily for some of us, society is reluctant to burn free thinkers at the stake. Besides, corporations are clamoring for flexible, self-directed problem solvers who know how to use technology effectively.

So what is our Baconian system to do? We must move quickly to reinvent schools around a Jeffersionian paradigm, or risk finding our educational institutions irrelevant to the future of our youth.

Getting Wired: Pragmatic Realities

If you're not jacked in, you're not part of the future.

— Bruce Sterling

The best way to truly grasp the power of educational telecomputing is to get on-line yourself and start exploring on your own. This section explores some of the mechanical details of this process including:

- Getting wired
- Hardware requirements
- Selecting a service
- Terminal software
- Additional utilities

While the general commentary applies to all computer platforms, the software descriptions are Macintosh specific. Most of the software referenced in this section is included on the accompanying CD-ROM.

Getting Wired

Depending on the networking capabilities at your site, there are several ways that your computer might be connected to the outside world. The most common (especially from classrooms and homes) is a direct connection to "plain old telephone service" (POTS). This is the slowest connection to use, but the easiest and cheapest to hook up. All the communication software on the accompanying CD-ROM *can* be used on POTS, but some of it probably shouldn't be. (We'll explain more later.)

Schools in some states, like California, are receiving support from the "Regional Bell Operating Companies" (RBOC's) for digital as opposed to analog (voice-grade) telephone lines. The most common of these services is called ISDN (Integrated Services Digital Network). The advantage of these lines is that, because they are designed for computer data, not voice, they operate at much higher data transfer rates. For example, the voice-grade phone line in your house can carry computer data at about a thousand characters per second — pretty fast if you are sending text, but sluggish for transferring color images. An ISDN line, by comparison, can carry data at over ten times that rate. Other types of digital service provide even faster data transfer rates limited only by your budget.

The costs associated with various phone services vary from region to region. Some services charge a flat monthly rate, and others (like the voice line in your house) are billed by time and mileage. Another cost factor to be considered is the interface needed to connect the phone line to your computer. Services operating over voice grade lines use inexpensive modems that cost a hundred dollars or less. The connection of your personal computer to a high-speed digital line will require more expensive interface hardware.

One way to make digital services more cost effective in school settings is to connect all the school's computers through a high-speed local area network (LAN) such as Ethernet. In addition to allowing all the computers on the site to exchange information, any of these machines can also be connected to a dedicated "server" that acts as a bridge to the outside high-speed digital line.

Once you move outside the range of a direct connection to a standard analog phone line, you will probably want help from your district's technology wizard, or from your local telephone service provider. As far as you are concerned, wiring should be the least of your responsibilities.

Before you run out and wire your buildings there are few other things to consider. For example, if the information service you plan to use is only accessible through dial-up access from a standard phone line, there is no sense in bringing in high-speed digital networks! Wiring and service selection need to be thought about at the same time.

What about Cable?

Interesting question. Most schools are provided with free basic cable service from the local cable TV provider. In addition to television programming, many of these services also provide access to X•Press X•Change: a high speed international newswire service that downloads the raw feeds from over a dozen wire services into your computer from your television cable. This service requires a special modem (called Infocipher) that is provided when you sign up for X•Press X•Change. For details, call 1-800-PC-NEWS.

X•Press X•Change is a wonderful service, but it is limited to one-way communication. In other words, you can get the live wire feeds, but you can't search the newswire databases. In an attempt to make life more interesting for the telephone companies, some cable services have decided to offer full two-way access to the Internet using a special cable modem (costing about $300). The interesting thing about this service is that it uses the TV cable you already have installed in your school or home, and — get this — it operates at about five times faster than an ISDN line! And that's just for starters. By 1995 Intel will be providing $300 cable modems that can receive data at *thirty million* bits per second — three times the speed of a standard Ethernet connection. While this modem will limit users to a 56Kb/sec "backchannel", this is still far faster than today's telephone-based modems.

If your local cable company hasn't rewired (or, more accurately, "reglassed") your community with the fiber optic lines needed to provide this service, get on their case! As with telephone lines, you'll need to check to see if the information services you want are available through the connections you are installing. At this stage, there are plenty of washed out bridges on the information highway.

Nuts and bolts; bits and bytes

Outfitting your computer to connect to information services requires a combination of hardware and software. We'll explore the software side of this task later. In all likelihood, you already have a perfectly good computer for connecting to most information services, especially if you are connecting over a standard phone line. The only extra expense is the modem.

A modem is a box (or internal circuit board) whose function is to take the computer's digital information (a string of 1's and 0's) and convert it to a series of beeping tones that can be sent down voice-grade lines. This process is called "modulating". Data sent (as tones) to your computer is then also converted back to digital strings of 1's and 0's so your computer can do something with this information. This process is called "demodulating". Put modulating and demodulating together, and you get "modem". (Pretty neat, eh?) Modems translate bits to beeps and beeps to bits. It's that easy.

Most high speed modems also handle other tasks including data compression, dialing the phone, sending faxes, waxing floors, etc. Fortunately, all this happens without you having to know the details.

In selecting a modem, my recommendation is to go for a combination of speed and price. As of mid-1994, modems that transmit at up to 19,200 baud cost about $100. (A "baud" is roughly equivalent to a bit of data per second, so a "19.2 modem" (as it is called) can pump data at a brisk rate.) Personally, this is what I am currently using.

Special note for cognoscenti: In reading 19.2 out loud, say "nineteen dot two". This makes you sound like a wizard. For extra credit, try this: "We're considering an ISDN line to a frame relay backbone, but the wire in our walls is lucky to handle POTS (say "pots") at 19.2."

If you still have any friends left after saying this, you should get out more often.

What if my service can't handle the speed?

Not to worry. Modems are great negotiators. When connecting to another modem, they sniff each other out, checking for the fastest data transfer speed at which they can mutually operate reliably, and (within a few seconds) make a choice. On regular phone lines, you'll almost never get the maximum speed out of your modem, just as you'll never get the maximum speed out of your car on regular roads. When you connect to an information service, you'll be told the fastest speed it can handle. By setting your modem to that speed, you'll get optimal performance most of the time.

If you know for a fact that the only telecommunications service you will use only operates at a slower speed (such as 2400 baud) then you can save some money and get a slower modem for about $25. Still, I'd opt for a faster one since all services are increasing their speeds as quickly as possible.

(Note that some information providers charge you more for the privilege of using speeds over 2400 baud, thus lending credence to the adage, "Tiempo es pesos".)

When you unpack your modem you'll find a cable connecting your modem to the computer, a phone line connecting the modem to a phone jack, and an incomprehensible manual outlining the calibration procedures for the Hubble space telescope.

Set the manual aside; you probably won't need it. Even if you do need it, you probably won't be able to make sense of it, so call your vendor if you need help.

Selecting a Service

OK, you have a phone line and the requisite hardware, now what?

While there are literally hundreds of valuable service providers for people interested in educational telecomputing, their services fall into three broad classes. It is likely that you'll start out with one service and add additional ones later to meet special needs.

In general, you can secure accounts with:

- Bulletin Board Systems (BBS's)
- Commercial on-line services
- Internet hosts

Each of these services offer something different.

Bulletin Boards

Anyone with a spare computer, a large hard disk and a spare phone line can set up a computer bulletin board. Generally (but not always) these BBS's are self-contained systems geared to a special interest group. Members typically connect to a BBS to post and read messages and to upload or download software or data files. Because most BBS's are self-contained, members can converse among themselves through the posting of messages or the sending of e-mail, but they cannot (in general) send mail to anyone without an account on the same system.

Because BBS's are easy to set up and maintain, they are ideal for community services. For example, a school or district can establish its own BBS for community use. Students can collaborate with classmates, and upload and download assignments. Teachers and parents can confer with each other through e-mail, and staff development materials can be posted for educators to explore at their own pace.

The general lack of connection between a BBS and the larger world of the Internet has good and bad properties associated with it.

First the good: The BBS is yours. You can maintain it just the way you want. You can determine exactly what kinds of material will be available, and to whom. You can start it up and shut it down anytime you want. You can restrict access to certain categories of users as you choose. If the system crashes, all the components are at your site so you can tend to them yourself.

Now for the bad news: The BBS is yours. You can maintain it just the way you want. You can determine exactly what kinds of material will be available, and to whom. You can start it up and shut it down anytime you want. You can restrict access to certain categories of users as you choose. If the system crashes, all the components are at your site so you can tend to them yourself.

 NovaLink

Because the number of BBS's is increasing at an exponential rate, it is quite possible that there is at least one educational BBS in your community you can explore. If you decide to set one up for yourself, you may want to try out the NovaLink software package from ResNova. This Mac-based software supports access from just about any computer system in your community. You can dial into it with simple text-based "terminal emulation" software, or you can use a nice graphical interface on the Mac. The choice is yours, and a full demonstration version of NovaLink is included on the CD-ROM.

Commercial On-line Services

While many commercial on-line services are available, in this section I'm focusing on proprietary telecommunications services such as America Online (AOL), Prodigy, GEnie, Applelink, e-World and Compuserve.

These services generally started out as huge commercial bulletin boards in the sense that they were self-contained. Some of them (Prodigy and AOL, for example) were geared from the start for non-technical users. Typically, new users are provided with the graphical user interface software and a few hours of use for free. Once the free-use period has expired, users are charged a monthly fee plus additional charges for special services or usage that exceeds the monthly allotment of time.

Educators represented by NEA can (at this writing) qualify for special discounts on AOL. For subscription information on any of the commercial services listed, call their toll-free numbers:

America Online 1-800-827-6364
Applelink 1-800-282-2732
e-World 1-800-775-4556
Compuserve 1-800-848-8990
GEnie 1-800-638-9636
Prodigy 1-800-776-3449

Once you get your startup kits, you are just a few minutes away from getting on-line!

What can I do with these services?
While the details vary from service to service, all the commercial on-line services provide the following:

- e-mail
- news and weather information
- software libraries

In addition, some of these services provide additional features including

- mail gateways to other services (allowing Compuserve users to send mail to people on AOL, or allowing AOL members to send mail to people on the Internet)
- gateways (usually limited) to popular Internet services such as newsgroups, "Gophers" and other resources scattered on thousands of computers located all over the planet

One of the features of a service like America Online (for example) is that it is very easy to use. Ease of use is important and accounts for the incredible growth in popularity of these services in the last two years.

Generally, there are two ways to gather information. You can forage for information by browsing around cyberspace, dipping into various data resources placed at your disposal. Or, if you know what you are looking for, you can enter a few keywords at the appropriate place and let the computer do the searching for you. Generally, you and your students will use a combination of these two strategies, depending on what you are seeking.

Largely because of ease of use and an increasingly rich library of information resources, commercial services like AOL make a great starting point for fledgling infonauts and cyberwizards alike. Even though I have accounts on several types of information services, I use AOL daily since I can log onto it with a local phone call from many cities in the United States or Canada.

Internet Hosts
The Internet is a huge network of networks that grew out of the Defense Advanced Research Projects Agency (DARPA) as a communications backbone for the United States in the event of all-out nuclear war. Data is pumped over the Net in the form of small packets that are each sent through the most efficient route to their destination where they are reassembled into their final form. This packet-switched network has expanded over the years to include most research universities in the world (through NSFNet) and is currently expanding at the rate of about 230 new nodes per hour. In June of 1969 there were three computers on the Net. By June of 1994 the number had jumped to three million.

Because the Net was created by and for the high tech research community using UNIX as an operating system on high-powered mainframes, ease of use was a secondary consideration. While you don't have to be a rocket scientist to use the Internet, many of its users are. This, coupled with the largely non-commercial nature of the Net has contributed to the slowness of the Internet to welcome mere mortals to its fold. Nonetheless, this is changing and, even if it weren't, the benefits of Net access far outweigh the cumbersome nature of access required if you are entering the Net with a simple terminal program using voice grade phone lines. (If you have direct access to the Net through a digital high-speed line, the Internet looks as pretty as any commercial service — even prettier in some respects. We'll explore that issue later.)

So why would I want to use the Internet?

Basically, once you are on the Net, you can easily gain access to information repositories located throughout the world. Interested in satellite weather maps of your area? No problem! You can get to them immediately. Want the latest images from Jupiter as it recovers from the direct hit of Shoemaker-Levy 9 comet? Easy! Just log onto the NASA computers and download all the images you want. Planning a trip to Guatemala? Drop in on the CIA databases and get the latest briefing papers. Curious about the Human Genome Project (and who isn't)? You can find it on the Net.

The truly neat thing about Net access is that the Internet doesn't care who you are. As long as you can type, information requests will be honored for Ph.D.'s and fourth-graders alike.

Net Access for Educators

Enlightened states have created statewide educational networks for use by educators and students. Unlike local bulletin boards, these networks offer a variety of services including education-specific resources applicable to specific states or districts along with access to the rest of the Internet world. Furthermore, these services are often seen as part of the state's responsibility for education and are made available for little or no direct cost to the users. SENDIT, the North Dakota educational network, charges about $1 per user per year for access to its system, for example.

If you live in a state that provides inexpensive or free telecommunications services for education, be sure you get an account on the service right away. If you don't have a statewide educational network where you live, petition the state to establish one. As Secretary of Education Richard Riley said in testimony to the United States Senate on May 25, 1994:

> It will be absolutely impossible to educate the coming generation of young people to high standards of excellence if their free access to and use of the NII (National Information Infrastructure) is seen as a secondary consideration to broad-based commercial purposes.
>
> ...
>
> Information that is too expensive to access will probably be information that is not used in the American classroom on a day-to-day basis. If the cost of using the NII is too high, if school children use it only on special assignments or hardly at all — then we undercut, at the very outset, one of the major reasons we are working so hard to create the Information Highway in the first place.
>
> In short, I believe that connecting up our schools and providing free usage — or usage that is at least as inexpensive as possible — is the right way to go.
>
> The principle of "free" public education for all children is the bedrock of our democracy. Not cheap, not inexpensive, not available for a fee — but in its very essence — "free". We believe in this basic American principle because we know its long-term value for society as a whole.
>
> A child or young person who gets an education of high standards and excellence becomes a dependable worker, a better citizen and a strong consumer. I believe that this way of thinking — about an early investment in education — should have broad application in creating a rate structure for the future use of the NII.

Educational institutions, large and small — schools, libraries, literacy centers, early childhood centers, community colleges and universities — should have total access and use of these services, as much as possible. If we can't connect the NII with all educational institutions at once, then schools, libraries, and literacy centers should be at the top of the list of public institutions that are rapidly linked to the Information Highway.

I believe that this early investment in education will provide a handsome and long-term economic return to business and to the Nation as a whole. For this is a good time, as a businessman once told me, to "smell the future" ... or to think long-term.

If we want to create a broad-based, well-educated work force that has the capacity to use information to keep our economy growing strong, then we need to hook this future work force into the NII early.

Once you are connected to your state's educational information service, you and your students will be able to conduct all kinds of research on every subject area imaginable.

Don't feel restricted to only one service — experiment until you find the combination of services that best fits your needs.

Internet Access

If you don't have access to a statewide educational connection to the Net, or have some other access point, you might be wondering how to get an Internet connection — especially if you are restricted to access through a voice-grade phone line. Fortunately, you have several options. A listing of public access dial-up services for the Internet (the PDial list) is provided on the CD-ROM. This listing is maintained by Peter Kaminsky and is updated periodically.

Two Internet services that you might want to explore right away are Delphi and the International Internet Association.

Delphi is a commercial Internet service provider that also maintains some services of its own (including human assistants when you get stuck.) Delphi is a commercial service that charges hourly rates, plus connection fees. All the basic Internet services are provided (given the limitation of dial-up lines).

The International Internet Association (IIA) has the goal of providing free Internet access to anyone who wants it. The IIA is a non-profit organization existing largely on private donations. Access to their services is provided through an 800 number. Unfortunately, the 800 number is not free — you have to pay for it. Even so, the fee is only about twenty cents per minute from anywhere in the United States, and access is available around the clock.

For more information on these two services, contact:

> Delphi 1-800-695-4005
> IIA (fax line)..1-202-387-5446

Before You Log On...
The vision of dipping into a vast sea of documents and programs in a highly democratic environment like the Internet is pretty heady stuff. So, before you go too far, it is important to know how to practice safe computing.

Yes, there are some pretty nasty characters on the Net whose idea of a good time is to entice you to download some innocuous program which comes with a nasty virus attached. A virus is a piece of software that comes connected to an application that you really want (like a word processor, for example). Once you start the program you intended to launch, the virus kicks in, attaching copies of itself to other programs, and then performing some prank on your computer — such as completely reformatting your hard disk when you aren't expecting it!

Virus authors give geeks a bad name. They apparently have nothing better to do than make life miserable for others and they should be made to stand in a corner until they grow up. Unfortunately, the "creativity" expressed by these vandals is hard to block.

How do you protect yourself? The good news is that excellent anti-virus software (such as the Disinfectant program on the enclosed CD-ROM) is available for free.

 Disinfectant

Disinfectant is one of the most popular anti-virus programs around. It is apparently a labor of love for John Norstad and his colleagues, and it gets updated whenever some new pathological strain of junk code emerges from the feeble mind of some pear-shaped dweeb whose only suntan comes from the glow of a CRT. The key to successful virus protection is to let Disinfectant check out your software BEFORE you run it for the first time. Ideally, you should download software to a floppy disk or other removable medium, and check it there first. Periodically, let Disinfectant take a look at your entire hard drive. You'll be glad you did.

Programs posted on commercial services such as America Online are generally checked for viruses first, so they are usually safe to play with, but I'd be careful with any program you grab from the millions of computers hanging on the Net. You're playing Russian Roulette with your computer.

Terminal Software

No matter what kind of network connection you have, you will need some software to let you access remote resources from the computer on your desk or lap. There are several ways to accomplish this, and these ways are dictated by the speed and nature of your network connection. The enclosed CD-ROM contains software for two types of connections: text-based "dumb terminal" emulation, and TCP/IP (Transfer Control Protocol/Internet Protocol) connections. (Don't worry about the alphabet soup, we'll get to all that in due course.)

If you subscribe to one of the commercial (and some non-commercial) services or bulletin boards, you will most likely be provided with special terminal software to facilitate your connection. In most cases, this software only works with one service. In other words, America Online's graphical user interface software works with their service only, as does Applelink's, or e-World's. Thought and care have gone into the design of these interface programs to make life as easy for you as possible.

For many other services, you'll be connecting your computer to the network as if it were a text-based terminal. This harkens back to the old days when Western Union teletype machines were used as computer terminals. As technology advanced, the noisy paper printers were replaced by terminals consisting of little more than text-based display screens and keyboards connected to modems. These terminals were called "glass teletypes" since they replicated the old mechanical monstrosities without the noise or waste of paper. One of the more popular versions of this terminal was made by Digital Equipment Corporation (DEC) and it was called the VT-100. The reason this history lesson is important is that, believe it or not, many network services still behave as if that is what people use today!

 ZTerm

Fortunately, it is easy to get your powerful color Macintosh with its plethora of fonts and styles to behave as if it were a brainless text-based terminal. The enclosed ZTerm software does a fine job! But, more importantly, ZTerm also supports the transfer of software from a remote computer to your personal hard disk drive. This file transfer ability (which works both ways) is very important, especially when you are downloading pictures, programs, or other files that are not represented by plain text. There are several protocols in popular use for the transfer of files from one computer to another. They differ mainly in the way the information is split into manageable chunks for sending, and on how errors are detected and corrected in the process. These protocols each have cryptic names — Xmodem, Ymodem, etc. You'll need to choose a protocol that is supported by the computer at the other end of your phone line. The Zmodem file transfer protocol is popular because it allows the transfer of a many files with one command, and because it synchronizes itself with the external computer quite nicely.

In addition to behaving like a glass teletype and supporting a few file transfer protocols (including Zmodem), ZTerm facilitates the connection process, even dialing the phone for you. ZTerm is shareware. This means that, if you use it, you should pay your shareware fee to the author. Instructions can be found in the ZTerm folder.

Why should I use a text-based terminal program?

Well, the real answer is because that is all some services support. Keep in mind that there are other computer platforms out there besides Macs, and some of them are pretty dreadful in the graphical user interface department. From the perspective of a service provider, a text-based connection is virtually guaranteed to work with anything you can connect to the Net — Apple II's, PC clones, Commodore 64's, you name it.

From your perspective, it isn't as bad as it seems, especially if you are operating over a voice grade telephone line with a modem speed of 14.4 kb/sec or less. At these speeds, text will burst onto your screen, but graphics would be ponderously slow to load as part of a continuously updated graphical interface. Using text-based menus you'll be able to navigate quickly around your service, identifying those items you might want to download for later reference. Your electronic mail (e-mail) is probably all text-based anyway, so there is no perceptual penalty there in any event.

When navigating around the Net, I view myself as a cybernaut journeying through the infosphere on a quest for information. I may or may not have a good map, although I generally will have a compass that points me in the direction I want to go. As I travel around, I find artifacts I want to bring home. These I place in my backpack to examine later when I am finished with my excursion. The map and compass refer to various navigational tools ranging from menus of choices to specific requests that I have made of the host computer. For example, (and we'll show how this is done later), I can ask for all references to Victor Hugo and be led to a collection of his works. At that point I might snag a copy of *Les Miserables* for myself that will be downloaded to my computer's hard drive (my backpack). Because I am paying for my time on the network, I want to get on, transact my business, and get off as quickly as possible. Once I am disconnected, I can examine the files I've collected at my leisure.

The thing I like about tools like ZTerm is that they provide a truly simple way to achieve my objectives and I can use them from virtually anywhere. I've logged on from hotel rooms, airport pay phones, and even from the new digital telephones available on some airplanes. While the interface is not elegant, ZTerm does the job. As you'll see when you open the folder, this program comes with extensive documentation and a richer set of features than you might think! If you are connecting to the Net from a regular phone line, this might be the way to go — especially if you have a slow (9600 baud or less) modem.

Me Tarzan, You Jane

Basically, your terminal software places all the power in the host computer, and treats your desktop machine like a prototypical network news anchor (body by Nautilus, brain by Mattel). The power resides remotely (in Jane, of course) while your powerful Macintosh sits there like some muscle-bound airhead.

Fortunately, there is an alternative to this sad state of affairs, and that is to unleash the power of your Macintosh as a full (if timid) player in the Internet world.

The key to this is that all Internet hosts obey a single protocol for the interchange of information. This protocol is called

TCP/IP, (Transfer Control Protocol/Internet Protocol). Any computer that obeys these rules can play with the big kids. Mainframes, high-end workstations, Macintoshes and IBM compatible computers can share information with each other using the same protocol!

 ## MacTCP

All you need to turn your Mac into a "real" player in the Internet world is an "init" file called MacTCP. This one tiny piece of software is essential in turning your Mac from a dumb terminal into an Einstein of the Internet.

Now that System 7.5 has been released, MacTCP is easy to get. (Just upgrade to System 7.5.) If you can't, or don't want to upgrade to System 7.5, you can purchase a license from Apple for this essential control panel from APDA (408-974-4667). Why does Apple charge to let your Mac behave like a Mac on the Internet? Beats me — you should ask Michael Spindler (1-408-996-1010).

 ## InterSLIP

As you shop around for Internet service providers (assuming you'll still be using your regular phone line, your service provider will probably ask you to set up a "SLIP" account allowing your dial-up access to mimic a dedicated Internet host. SLIP stands for Serial Line Internet Protocol, and it needs an init of its own called InterSLIP. (I've included it on the CD-ROM.)

The better way to go is with a genuine high-speed digital connection between your Macintosh and the Internet. Pacific Bell has offered to bring such lines into all California schools for free, and to waive the first year's usage fee! GTE has also initiated a special educational program in California. Schools in their service area are being offered $2,000 usage credit along with free consulting to help them pick the service best meeting their needs.

Once you have connected to high-speed digital lines, you'll never want to go back to your regular phone line. For information on services like ISDN, Frame Relay, and other pipelines that Alexander Graham Bell never thought about when he called Watson for help, contact your local phone company. Tell them I sent you.

In the meantime, all is not lost. You can still benefit from the TCP/IP connection with your current phone line if you have a 14.4 (or faster) modem and a modicum of patience.

In any event, know that setting your system up to play in the major leagues may require the help of a local expert who understands all the technical ramifications of your computer and its relationship to your network. I can boil water, but I don't make soufflés.

Now that you've added two inits to the pile you've already got on your Mac, and you've signed up to play with the pros, what's next?

For starters, you can kiss that purely text-based Internet access software good-bye! You can create and use multi-media hypertext-based information browsers that let you navigate the hot spots of the World Wide Web with tools like Mosaic or MacWeb. You can actually use the traditional Mac interface to select and download Net-based software as if it were resident on your own local area network using tools like Fetch and TurboGopher. Basically, MacTCP and InterSLIP let your Mac behave on the network like a Macintosh instead of like some wimpy antique with a pathetic, text-based interface.

While we're on the topic of inits, there are a couple of more from Apple that you should have in your System folder at all times.

QuickTime

QuickTime is an Apple-supplied init that lets you work with QuickTime movies and with images compressed using the JPEG standard (more on that later.) You probably received QuickTime with your computer, but you should check to see if you have the latest version. At the time this book was being written, QuickTime 2.0 was nearing completion. This init is an essential component of any Net-based activity involving multimedia. To start with, you can't view movies or JPEG images without it, and JPEG images are so compact that you'll want to use that format a lot for sending image files to others on the Net.

 Thread Manager

This init is needed to run Sparkle, the MPEG movie player included on the CD-ROM. Threads allow programs to be split into pieces that each run separately, letting the program perform many tasks at once. This capability is unleashed on your Mac if the Thread Manager init is dropped into your System folder.

 Mosaic

One of the hottest pieces of software used for browsing the Web is a program called Mosaic. This program is becoming so popular these days that Mosaic users mingle by themselves at cocktail parties. Those parties are getting pretty big these days. In August of 1994, more than 1600 copies of Mosaic were downloaded from the main archive per day. And this doesn't count the number that are downloaded from other sources or made available to people on CD-ROM's. (You're welcome.) Best of all, it's free!

Basically, this program functions a lot like hypermedia authoring tools that allow you to create documents with lots of media elements (e.g., text, images, sounds, movies, and other programs). By clicking on various objects, you can branch to other areas of the same application, or can leap to different applications. (DOCMaker is an example of a program of this type provided on the accompanying CD-ROM).

The main difference between Mosaic and these other programs is that, rather than being constrained to your local disk drive, Mosaic button clicks can reach pretty much anywhere on the Internet for data.

The key to this is something called the World Wide Web, or WWW for short. WWW was created by scientists at CERN (a heavy-duty science lab) in Switzerland as a way to bring some coherence to navigation on the Internet without restricting access in any way (a very Swiss thing to do, actually). The Web is navigated with the aid of "browsers". Browsers are programs that interpret scripts written in an arcane language called HTML (for Hypertext Markup Language) that we will describe shortly. These text-based scripts are turned into pretty displays when interpreted by programs like Mosaic.

A Mosaic screen looks like a good Macintosh document — different font sizes are used for headers, graphics appear in full color along with the text, and sounds and QuickTime movies can be played from within the document. The truly interesting thing about Mosaic documents is that two pictures appearing side by side may be downloaded automatically from sources on opposite sides of the planet. As a viewer of a document, you needn't know nor care where the various media elements come from. In this respect, Mosaic keeps you focused on the content, not on the mechanics of finding the material you want to see.

This comes at a price, however. If you want to browse Mosaic documents with embedded images, you'll find your fastest modem to appear sluggish if you are limited to POTS. On the other hand, if you have an ISDN line or other high-speed digital connection to the Net, you'll feel as if the whole world of information is literally at your fingertips. The difference between Mosaic and a text-based terminal program is like the difference between a Macintosh and MS-DOS.

MacWeb

Other Web browsers exist besides Mosaic. One of the newer ones that looks promising is called MacWeb. Basically, MacWeb is a lot like Mosaic, except that it uses less memory. Try both and choose the one you like best. Unless you have heaps of RAM to spare, MacWeb will probably be your browser of choice. (MacWeb is also free!)

HTML Edit

Web browsers rely on scripts written in HTML — a markup language that uses special marks to indicate type styles, pictures, hypertext links and other objects that make the Web such a multimedia delight to explore. The reason for using special marks instead of the various styles themselves is that the resulting documents are pure text, allowing them to be transmitted through anyone's e-mail system and loaded onto anyone's computer. It also guarantees that these documents will work with browsers on any computer system. Mosaic documents that work on your Macintosh will also work on a UNIX workstation. That's the good news.

The bad news is that HTML documents look pretty cryptic. Fortunately, there is an HTML authoring tool that places all the special marks for you with a simple click of the mouse. This program, HTML Edit, is on the CD-ROM.

MacHTTP

My guess is that you'll start your Web experience by using Mosaic or MacWeb to navigate through documents created by others. Next, you'll try your hand at creating some documents of your own using HTML Edit. But, if you're really brave, you'll want to create your own WWW node. To do this, you'll need to turn your Mac into an Internet site and install an HTTP server. This would give you the coolest bulletin board in town, if you're game enough to try!

 Fetch

I don't want to create the impression that the only reason for getting a SLIP account is so you can browse the Web. Once you become a full-fledged Internet citizen, all aspects of Net access improve. While file transfer, document searches, and e-mail can be handled with text-based terminals, you'll want to use Mac-like environments whenever possible.

Fetch is a program that makes it easy for you to download images, programs, and other files from computers scattered all over the Internet. Instead of requiring a lengthy series of text commands to initiate file transfers, Fetch brings point and click simplicity to this essential task.

 Turbo Gopher

Turbo Gopher is a program that, like Fetch, brings a Mac-like face to the Internet when you go searching for resources scattered all over the place. It requires a SLIP account as well. Technically, a gopher site is an Internet destination that has organized information into a hierarchical menu. By maneuvering through the menus, you can find the information you are looking for quite easily. Through the use of a search program called Veronica, the entire Net can be searched for any topic of interest to you and, within a few seconds, a custom menu of choices based on your request will be built for you to navigate! (The next chapter describes this process in some detail.)

 Eudora

Eudora is a heavy-duty e-mail program that will simplify your life, especially if you receive a LOT of mail every day and have a SLIP account. The Eudora manual is quite large, but the many features of this program are worth exploring!

 Maven

The Net is not limited to the transfer of text and images. You can also talk to others over the Internet if you have a high-speed line (ISDN or better) and a program called Maven. Netiquette requires that you be careful when using the Net in place of a voice telephone. Digitized voice takes a lot of bandwidth, even when it is compressed. Be gentle! Be brief!

 CU-See Me

And, as long as you are sending voice, why not add your moving image to the message? Cornell University's CU-SeeMe product lets you chat with other Net users and see their images at the same time they see yours — two-way television on the Internet! All you need is an AV Macintosh, or one with a video input card and a video camera. (Plus a SLIP account or a high speed digital connection to the Net.)

As with Maven, be thrifty. Bandwidth is *becoming* free, but we aren't there yet!

Basically, I included Maven and CU-SeeMe so you can get a glimpse of where the Net is heading. Most of us are limited to text-based telecommunications today, but that world is changing rapidly!

Additional Utilities

Ever since the Tower of Babel we've had a hard time communicating with others. Languages sprouted up all over the world, and the task of translating between them has been formidable. This is also the case for computers. Each platform has its own way of representing information, and even different products designed to run on the same computer handle information in different ways. If you've ever tried to open a document written in one word processor with another piece of software, you might have experienced some of the challenges that are multiplied on the Net where access is provided to just about every computer platform known on the planet.

Fortunately, some semblance of order has emerged over the years, both in the form of data stored on the Net, and in the representations of various objects (such as sounds, color pictures, and movies). The utilities on the enclosed CD-ROM provide a Rosetta Stone of sorts for converting and using files created in a variety of formats. With any luck, you'll find that just about any document you download will be readable with the software we've provided.

Before getting to document specific translation (such as that between different graphics formats), we'll explore the more basic issues of conversion having to do with text and binary files.

In the Internet world, everything is stored as either text or binary files. Text files consist of collections of characters found in plain text — the upper and lower case alphabet, numbers, and punctuation marks. These characters can be read by and displayed on any computer. Binary files, on the other hand, are made from collections of 8-bit characters of which only some are text. Binary files generally represent pictures, sounds, computer software, formatted documents (like a Microsoft Word file), and anything that can't be represented by readable text. Unlike text files, binary files are often platform specific.

Since terminal programs (like ZTerm) can transfer either kind of file to or from your computer, there is no problem, generally, in shipping both types of files over the Net. Problems do arise, however, if you want to send a file to a friend using e-mail. In this case, your e-mail program will most likely expect text only — no fancy binary whiz-bangs allowed! The solution to this problem is to translate your binary file into a form that can be represented in pure text, cross your fingers, and then hope that the person receiving it can translate it back again.

Fortunately, there are two commonly used translation methods for achieving this task, and they work across platforms. In other words, I can do a text translation of a color picture on a UNIX machine, send it to an MS-DOS computer, have that file transferred to an Apple II, and then move it to a Macintosh for translation into a form that my Mac software will gladly accept! The two translation systems in common use are called "HQX" and "UUEncode". Both of these are used to convert binary files to text representations, and to convert them back again. The text-based representations are a bit longer than their binary counterparts, but these translation strategies are worth their weight in gold.

 UULite

UULite lets you convert binary files to special text files and convert them back again. You'll find this method of file conversion used a lot for pictures, sounds and movies, but not (generally) for programs. The way to tell you are looking at a UUEncoded file is that each line starts with an "M" followed by a string of letters and numbers. The neat thing about UUEncoded files is that you can place comments at the start of your document designed to be read by the recipient before he or she converts the file back to binary form. For example, you might preface a picture with a description of the artwork, a request for comments, etc. Once UULite starts working on the file, all these comments are ignored and you're left with a traditional binary file. Pretty neat, eh?

Since some e-mail systems restrict file length per message, UULite will automatically break your file into as many parts as needed to keep the size of each file under the limit for your system. Once all the parts are downloaded, UULite can assemble them back into one large text file before automatically decoding them. My guess is that you'll use this program a lot!

HQXer

The other text-based binary file format you're likely to encounter is called HQX. This is often the format used for executable code (what we mortals call computer programs). There are lots of programs that deal efficiently with the conversion to this format and back again. In addition to HQXer, you'll find this capability supported by Compact Pro (where the format is called BinHex, just to keep you on your toes.)

Drop•PS

Sometimes you'll find documents on the Net that are saved as PostScript files in order to preserve formatting, graphics, etc. If you want to print these out, it's handy to have a utility like Drop•PS on your desktop. Just gather up one of more PostScript files and drop them over the Drop•PS icon, and they will be sent to your laser printer.

Common Ground MiniViewer

Another popular way to share highly formatted documents with people who don't have the same software you used to create the document is to "print" them to the Common Ground file format. Common Ground is a commercial product, but the

Common Ground MiniViewer is free for you to use in viewing and printing these documents. Generally, Common Ground files have ".dp" at the end. And no, I don't know why.

Pictures...

One of the things that must make telephone executives smile in their dreams is the large number of color images scattered in repositories all over the Net, just waiting for some hapless cybernaut to transfer them with a pokey 2400 baud modem.

While images exist in numerous formats, two of the more popular are called GIF images and JPEG images. Both types of files are compressed renditions of the original that get expanded when viewed or edited. The GIF format was created by Compuserve and is designed for 8-bit (256 color) images. As this format became popular, it migrated to other systems, and is now the virtual standard for distributing 8-bit color images on the Net.

The JPEG (Joint Photography Experts Group) format works with just about any color or black and white image, including those with millions of colors (32-bit images). Depending on the quality you want, JPEG images can be compressed by incredible amounts and still look pretty good when expanded for viewing. Generally, JPEG images are more compact than their GIF counterparts, but you'll find both on the Net. On occasion you'll even find uncompressed image files, but it is considered bad form to ship these around because they eat up hard disk space, and they plug up the pipeline when they are moved from one site to another.

 GraphicConverter

If your goal is to convert an image from one format to another, or to open one of the industrial-strength graphics formats, such as TIFF images, then GraphicConverter is your tool. This incredible program not only supports image display and file conversion, it also lets you edit pictures, change their resolution, size, and color range, and — get this — supports some of the fancy image manipulation tasks associated with high-priced commercial offerings like PhotoShop. This tool is on every Macintosh I own. We'll have more to say about this program later!

 EasyPlay

In your explorations of the Net, you'll come across QuickTime movies. Apple provides a basic player program with QuickTime called Simple Player that lets you view these movies, but I prefer using a shareware program called Easy Play for this task. This program plays the movie centered on a full-screen background, and also lets you build catalogs of all the film clips on your disk. We'll have more to say about this program in the Powertools chapter.

 Sparkle

Suppose, however, that you want to see a movie recorded in the MPEG (Motion Picture Experts Group) format. In that case, Sparkle will do the job and, if you wish, convert an MPEG movie to QuickTime so you can incorporate it into multimedia applications that expect all movies to have the QuickTime format. In addition to bridging the major formats of digital movies, the documentation for Sparkle provides a great description of how movie compression is accomplished.

 SoundApp

SoundApp plays or converts sound files dropped onto it. (Just drag any sound file onto the SoundApp icon and it will do the rest.) You can choose the file format you want for conversion by launching SoundApp and setting the preferences.

Just about any sound format you are likely to encounter on the Net is supported: SoundEdit, AIFF, AIFF-C, System 7 sounds, Sun Audio (AU files), NeXT, snd, Windows WAV, Sound Blaster VOC, Amiga MOD, Amiga IFF, Sound Designer II, DVI ADPCM, and others. Based on the preferences you have set, these sounds can be converted into System 7 sound, sound suitcase, AIFF, WAV and NeXT formats. Not bad for a free program!

 UlawPlay

If you just want to play UNIX (AU) sound files, Ulaw Play is all you'll need.

Compression Tools

While we all want the phone companies to be profitable, there's no sense tying up your phone line any longer than necessary. If you can't spring for a high speed digital line, you can make file transfers more efficient by compressing them first. Unlike most image compression algorithms (like JPEG), file compression is lossless — no information is thrown away. While each compression program has its own strategies for squishing the air out of files, the net results are pretty similar. Pure text or word processor documents usually compress to half their original size. Hypercard stacks compress by a lot, as do many programs.

Even though file compression adds some steps to file transfer, it is worth the effort. Compressed files take a lot less time to transmit.

Note: If you want to send a file in a pure text format (UUEncoded, or HQX'ed) be sure to compress the file first, *then* convert it to a pure text format. Also, as a courtesy, be sure to make it easy for the file's recipient to know what you have done. Adding letters to the end of your filename is the best way to do this. For example, when I see a file on the Net called something like "gribble.cpt.hqx" I know (from my many minutes of experience) that I must work from right to left in decoding it after it has been downloaded. The "hqx" part lets me know that I need to convert it from a text file to binary first. Then the "cpt" part tells me that it has been compressed with Compact Pro, and that my next step is to uncompress it. At that point I'll have an uncompressed file on my hard drive called "gribble" that may or may not have been worth the effort to download.

 Compact Pro

Compact Pro is one of my personal favorite pieces of shareware. It compresses anything from single files to folders full of programs and documents and provides the option of allowing the compressed file to "autoexpand" when opened. Even though it makes the resulting file a tad larger that it would be otherwise, I always opt for the autoexpand option as a courtesy to others who might not have had your foresight to hang out with a gracious (if balding) author who made the Compact Pro shareware available to them on an enclosed CD-ROM. (Let's not mention names, shall we?)

In addition to data compression and expansion, Compact Pro is two, two products in one. It also lets you "binhex" or "unbinhex" those "hqx" files, saving you the trouble of opening two applications. Files compressed with Compact Pro often have ".cpt" at the end of their names.

 Stuffit Expander

Aside from a product name that should not be muttered in anger, Stuffit has achieved a great measure of enthusiastic support from Net users. You'll find lots of Stuffit documents on the Net, and Stuffit Expander is a "freeware" package that will let you expand them yourself. One particularly nice feature of this product is that it will automatically "unbinhex" an "hqx'ed" archive before expanding it.

This program also supports the expansion of other formats (e.g., Compact Pro), but the power of this tool is really unleashed when you use the Expander Enhancer features accompanying the shareware package, DropStuff. This program not only lets you compress files, but also enhances the ability of Stuffit Expander to expand and decode a wide variety of file formats including Applelink "packages", UUEncoded files, and several more formats supported by UNIX-based computers and other platforms lurking on the Net.

File compression can be automated to include conversion to "binhex" files that can be transmitted to others through e-mail. Once you've set your preferences, you can just drag a collection of files on top of the DropStuff icon, and let it do the rest automatically. You can even encrypt your compacted files, and save them as self-extracting archives to send to your friends who don't have Stuffit Expander. This is one powerful shareware package, and I know you have your checkbook handy to reward the authors for a job well done! Files compressed with Stuffit often have ".sit" at the end of their names.

 ZipIt

If you've ever spent time in the world of MS-DOS, you've likely encountered "zipped" files compressed with a program called PKZip. The expander, PKunZiP is free, but only runs on Intel-based platforms. As it turns out, there are lots of great documents on the Net created with the expectation that users will be running Intel-based computers, and we Mac users need a way to pry our way into those documents to see what they contain.

ZipIt does just that. Not only can you expand "zipped" files, you can create them for transmittal to your brethren (and sistren) who have yet to see the wisdom of your platform choice. Files compressed in this format often have ".zip" at the end of their names.

Goalposts Along the Information Highway

The Goals 2000: Educate America Act was signed into law on March 31, 1994. This act serves as a template for the redefinition of educational practice in the United States with the goal of insuring that all students are prepared for life in the 21st century. As Labor Secretary Robert Reich stated in a press conference on February 22, 1994;

> I see everyday the relationship between what you earn and what you learn. In fact, today, education doesn't end at the age of 18 or 16 or even, for those who go into college, at the age of 22. Education must be a lifelong process.

Among industrialized nations we have one of the best systems of higher education in the world, but among the worst systems for getting young people from school to work. [There is] a widening gap between those who are well educated and those who are less educated in terms of earnings. That gap is widening year by year. It's been widening for fifteen years because there is greater and greater demand for skilled people, but less and less demand for people with less skills, for relatively unskilled labor.

If we've learned anything from the past recession, and now the recovery, it's that the old jobs are not coming back. [We propose] a fundamentally new approach to the most valuable resource in our economy — and that is, to use a cold-blooded term, human capital. Every other resource in America moves easily across borders these days — technology, money, factories and equipment can be put anywhere. The one relatively immobile resource upon which our future uniquely depends is the capacity of our people to innovate.

The world has undergone many changes in the past few years, and our educational system needs to respond to those changes. One change with profound implications for education as well as for society at large is the advent of the communication age — an era brought about by the rapid increase of communication bandwidth and the increase in information access that will soon be available to anyone, anywhere, at any time. A cornerstone of this new era in the United States is the National Information Infrastructure (NII). The NII promises to have an impact on how we work, learn, and entertain ourselves. It promises to improve almost all aspects of our lives.

It is in the area of education that the NII will have a most profound effect — an effect being felt already in states where learners and educators have access to online services through a combination of commercial and non-commercial providers. The services available today are invaluable, and they will only get better as bandwidth increases, and the number and nature of educational offerings expands.

A major impact of the NII in education is that the role of the educator will be transformed. No longer will educators need to be the prime deliverers of "facts". Instead, educators can become more like "field guides" as they and their students explore vast domains of knowledge together, using the Net as their trail through the world of information. Learners and educators who use the NII to facilitate lifelong learning will be well-prepared for their future.

This chapter is an attempt to show how currently available Internet-based information resources can be applied to the eight objectives of Goals 2000. The suggestions are by no means comprehensive since a current list of educational resources on the Net would be huge, and new resources are being added daily. The Internet is growing by about 230 new hosts per hour. Our goal, then, is to show a few of the many resources that you can use to help incorporate the eight national goals into your daily practice.

If all this talk about "information superhighways" has your head spinning, take heart. The prime directive of the Internet is "Ask; someone knows." As long as you are willing to dip your toe in the informational ocean that can be accessed with your personal computer from your local telephone, you'll soon be surfing effortlessly over vast seas of information that will make textbooks look like antiques!

Goals 2000 Highlights

The Goals 2000: Educate America Act describes a set of national education goals. The following is an overview of these goals and the Congressional mandate regarding educational technology. Since the entire Goals 2000 Act is over two hundred pages long, I'm only including some highlights in this section.

The Act is built around eight specific goals:

1. School Readiness
By the year 2000, all children in America will start school ready to learn.

Objectives:
- All children will have access to high-quality and developmentally appropriate preschool programs that help prepare children for school;

- Every parent in the United States will be a child's first teacher and devote time each day to helping such parent's preschool child learn, and parents will have access to the training and support parents need; and

- Children will receive the nutrition, physical activity experiences, and health care needed to arrive at school with healthy minds and bodies, and to maintain the mental alertness necessary to be prepared to learn, and the number of low-birthweight babies will be significantly reduced through enhanced prenatal health systems.

2. *School Completion*

By the year 2000, the high school graduation rate will increase to at least 90 percent.

Objectives:
- The Nation must dramatically reduce its school dropout rate, and 75 percent of the students who do drop out will successfully complete a high school degree or its equivalent;

- The gap in high school graduation rates between American students from minority backgrounds and their non-minority counterparts will be eliminated.

3. *Student Achievement and Citizenship*

By the year 2000, all students will leave grades 4, 8, and 12 having demonstrated competency over challenging subject matter including English, mathematics, science, foreign languages, civics and government, economics, arts, history, and geography, and every school in America will ensure that all students learn to use their minds well, so they may be prepared for responsible citizenship, further learning, and productive employment in our Nation's modern economy.

Objectives:
- The academic performance of all students at the elementary and secondary level will increase significantly in every quartile, and the distribution of minority students in each quartile will more closely reflect the student population as a whole;

- The percentage of all students who demonstrate the ability to reason, solve problems, apply knowledge, and write and communicate effectively will increase substantially;

- All students will be involved in activities that promote and demonstrate good citizenship, good health, community service, and personal responsibility;

- All students will have access to physical education and health education to ensure they are healthy and fit;

- The percentage of all students who are competent in more than one language will substantially increase; and

- All students will be knowledgeable about the diverse cultural heritage of this Nation and about the world community.

4. *Teacher Education and Professional Development*

By the year 2000, the Nation's teaching force will have access to programs for the continued improvement of their professional skills and the opportunity to acquire the knowledge and skills needed to instruct and prepare all American students for the next century.

Objectives:
- All teachers will have access to preservice teacher education and continuing professional development activities that will provide such teachers with the knowledge and skills needed to teach to an increasingly diverse student population with a variety of educational, social, and health needs;

- All teachers will have continuing opportunities to acquire additional knowledge and skills needed to teach challenging subject matter and to use emerging new methods, forms of assessment, and technologies;

- States and school districts will create integrated strategies to attract, recruit, prepare, retrain, and support the continued professional development of teachers, administrators, and other educators, so that there is a highly talented work force of professional educators to teach challenging subject matter; and

82

- Partnerships will be established, whenever possible, among local educational agencies, institutions of higher education, parents, and local labor, business, and professional associations to provide and support programs for the professional development of educators.

5. *Mathematics and Science*

By the year 2000, United States students will be first in the world in mathematics and science achievement.

Objectives:
- Mathematics and science education, including the metric system of measurement, will be strengthened throughout the system, especially in the early grades;

- The number of teachers with a substantive background in mathematics and science, including the metric system of measurement, will increase by 50 percent; and

- The number of United States undergraduate and graduate students, especially women and minorities, who complete degrees in mathematics, science, and engineering will increase significantly.

6. *Adult Literacy and Lifelong Learning*

By the year 2000, every adult American will be literate and will possess the knowledge and skills necessary to compete in a global economy and exercise the rights and responsibilities of citizenship.

Objectives:
- Every major American business will be involved in strengthening the connection between education and work;

- All workers will have the opportunity to acquire the knowledge and skills, from basic to highly technical, needed to adapt to emerging new technologies, work methods, and markets through public and private educational, vocational, technical, workplace, or other programs;

- The number of quality programs, including those at libraries, that are designed to serve more effectively the needs of the growing number of part-time and mid-career students will increase substantially;

- The proportion of the qualified students, especially minorities, who enter college, who complete at least two years, and who complete their degree programs will increase substantially;

- The proportion of college graduates who demonstrate an advanced ability to think critically, communicate effectively, and solve problems will increase substantially; and

- Schools, in implementing comprehensive parent involvement programs, will offer more adult literacy, parent training and life-long learning opportunities to improve the ties between home and school, and enhance parents' work and home lives.

7. *Safe, Disciplined, and Alcohol and Drug-Free Sschools*
By the year 2000, every school in the United States will be free of drugs, violence, and the unauthorized presence of firearms and alcohol and will offer a disciplined environment conducive to learning.

Objectives:
- Every school will implement a firm and fair policy on use, possession, and distribution of drugs and alcohol;

- Parents, businesses, governmental and community organizations will work together to ensure the rights of students to study in a safe and secure environment that is free of drugs and crime, and that schools provide a healthy environment and are a safe haven for all children;

84

- Every local educational agency will develop and implement a policy to ensure that all schools are free of violence and the unauthorized presence of weapons;

- Every local educational agency will develop a sequential, comprehensive kindergarten through twelfth grade drug and alcohol prevention education program;

- Drug and alcohol curriculum should be taught as an integral part of sequential, comprehensive health education;

- Community-based teams should be organized to provide students and teachers with needed support; and

- Every school should work to eliminate sexual harassment.

8. *Parental Participation*

By the year 2000, every school will promote partnerships that will increase parental involvement and participation in promoting the social, emotional, and academic growth of children.

Objectives:
- Every State will develop policies to assist local schools and local educational agencies to establish programs for increasing partnerships that respond to the varying needs of parents and the home, including parents of children who are disadvantaged or bilingual, or parents of children with disabilities;

- Every school will actively engage parents and families in a partnership which supports the academic work of children at home and shared educational decision making at school; and

- Parents and families will help to ensure that schools are adequately supported and will hold schools and teachers to high standards of accountability.

What About Technology?

These eight goals form the framework for the transformation of educational practice requested by the Federal government. Educational technology is seen as an essential tool for the achievement of these goals. In particular, the Goals 2000 Act provides leadership at the Federal level, through the Department of Education, by developing a national vision and strategy to:

- Infuse technology and technology planning into all educational programs and training functions carried out within school systems at the State and local level;

- Coordinate educational technology activities among the related Federal and State departments or agencies, industry leaders, and interested educational and parental organizations;

- Establish working guidelines to ensure maximum interoperability nationwide and ease of access for the emerging technologies so that no school system will be excluded from the technological revolution;

- Ensure that Federal technology-related policies and programs facilitate the use of technology in education;

- Promote awareness of the potential of technology for improving teaching and learning;

- Support State and local efforts to increase the effective use of technology for education;

- Demonstrate ways in which technology can be used to improve teaching and learning, and to help ensure that all students have an equal opportunity to meet State education standards;

- Ensure the availability and dissemination of knowledge (drawn from research and experience) that can form the basis for sound State and local decisions about investment in, and effective uses of, educational technology;

- Promote high-quality professional development opportunities for teachers and administrators regarding the integration of technology into instruction and administration;

- Promote the effective uses of technology in existing Federal education programs, such as Chapter 1 of Title I of the Elementary and Secondary Education Act of 1965 and vocational education programs; and

- Monitor, advancements in technology to encourage the development of effective educational uses of technology.

These are ambitious goals. They represent a clear mandate, and a challenge to all who have an interest in the education of our youth. The connection between the eight goals and technology, specifically the connection with communications-based technologies such as the Internet, is quite strong. The following sections provide a starting point for making the connection between the education goals and existing communication technologies.

The Internet

The Internet is often thought of as the starting point for the NII. This network of networks is growing at a rate of 15% per month, and reaches to the remote corners of the globe through a combination of fiberoptic, copper and wireless connections.

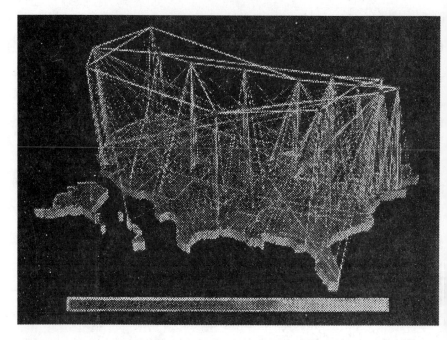

This picture (downloaded from the Electronic Frontier Foundation's database) shows a snapshot of some of the linkages holding this web together.

ERIC

While there is no "one stop shopping" destination for educational materials on the Internet, ERIC comes close.

The Educational Resources Information Center (ERIC) is a federally funded, nationwide information network designed to provide you with ready access to educational literature.

At the heart of ERIC is the largest education database in the world containing more than 800,000 records of journal articles, research reports, curriculum and teaching guides, conference papers, and books. Each year, approximately 30,000 new records are added. The ERIC database is available in many formats at hundreds of locations. ERIC presents education information in a format convenient to users. More than twenty years ago, ERIC became the first commercial online database. In 1986 the ERIC database became available for searching on CD-ROM. Now ERIC is at the forefront of efforts to make education information available through computer networks. ERIC is available to thousands of teachers, administrators, parents, students, and others through electronic networks including the Internet, CompuServe, America Online, and other online services. Network users can read and download information on the latest education trends and issues. On some systems, users can direct education-related questions to AskERIC and get a response from an education specialist within forty-eight hours. ERIC also offers customized assistance through a network of subject-specific education clearinghouses that provide toll-free reference and referral and free or low-cost publications on important education topics. The ERIC system, managed by the U.S. Department of Education, Office of Educational Research and Improvement (OERI), consists of sixteen Clearinghouses, a number of adjunct Clearinghouses, and additional support components. The ERIC Clearinghouses collect, abstract, and index education materials for the ERIC database; respond to requests for information in their subject areas; and produce special publications on current research, programs, and practices.

Access to ERIC is often provided directly by Internet or commercial network providers. If you can't find the ERIC databases easily, you'll be able to find them using a program described later — Veronica.

Other Services
In our list of services, I focused primarily on resources that can be accessed through a program called "Gopher" (more on this later), "ftp" (File Transfer Protocol) and on "listservs" and "Usenet newsgroups".

Gophers
A "gopher site" is a computer system whose files can be listed and transferred through the Gopher program. This program displays a menu of choices showing the various files, images,

programs, or other resources available to you. By moving the screen cursor to the desired entry and pressing the Return key, the chosen item is displayed on your screen. If you want a copy of the item, Gopher has commands that will transfer the file from the remote site to your personal computer. The metaphor I like to use is that of a bag I carry with me on my trip through cyberspace. As I uncover things that catch my fancy, I snag them and place them in my bag to examine later (when I am off-line).

One of the challenges in using Gopher is knowing where to "go fer" information. It is highly unlikely that you will know (or care!) which computer system you need to access for a copy of Jefferson's autobiography, for example. Fortunately, you don't need to know that information as long as you have access to another program called Veronica. Usually offered by the service you use to gain access to the Internet, Veronica lets you search for information by entering a descriptive word, phrase or title. For example, if you were to ask Veronica to find references to "Thomas Jefferson", within about 10 seconds or so any gopher site in the world with an entry on Thomas Jefferson will have responded and you would see something like the following list on your screen :

```
        Internet Gopher Information Client 2.0 pl10

    High-Level Search of Gopher Menus (no field searching):
Thomas Jefferson

        1.   0214 Thomas Jefferson University
[gopher.cc.umanitoba.ca]/
        2.   Papers of Thomas Jefferson
[gopher.pupress.princeton.edu]/
        3.   Papers of Thomas Jefferson, Second Series
[gopher.pupress.princeto../
        4.   Thomas Jefferson [gopher.vt.edu]/
        5.   Thomas Jefferson Library Gopher (Gopher)
[mercury.cs.umsl.edu]/
        6.   Thomas Jefferson Library Gopher (Gopher)
[umslvma.umsl.edu]/
        7.   Thomas Jefferson Univ (jeflin.tju.edu)
~[jeflin.tju.edu 70 GUSPA D../
```

8. Thomas Jefferson Univ (pinkslip.tju.edu)
~[pinkslip.tju.edu 70 GUS../
9. Thomas Jefferson Univ ~[tjgopher.tju.edu 70 CR
GUSPA D930613] [tjg../
10. Thomas Jefferson University Catalog
[gopher.library.upenn.edu]/
11. Thomas Jefferson University [jeflin.tju.edu] <TEL>
12. 940209 Thomas Jefferson High School for Science &
Technology.. <HTML>

By choosing one of the items in the menu and pressing the Enter
key, you will see a list of items in the chosen directory.

```
                    Internet Gopher Information Client 2.0
pl10

                         Thomas Jefferson [gopher.vt.edu]

     1. A Summary View Of The Rights Of British America
(summary).
     2. Addresses, Messages, And Replies (address).
     3. Autobiography (autobio).
     4. Indian Addresses (indians).
     5. Jefferson's First Inaugural Address (inaugurl).
     6. Letters (letters).
     7. Miscellany (miscella).
     8. Notes On The State Of Virginia (virginia).
     9. Public Papers (public_p).
```

Any of these documents could then be downloaded to your
computer using Gopher's download command and your
communications software.

That's all there is to it! And, if you use a service with a
graphical user interface, it is even easier.

One of the Gopher services of tremendous value to education is
the Gopher Jewels, a catalog of selected gopher sites arranged
by category. Gopher sites are placed in particular categories as
a result of finding related information buried somewhere in
their "hole". This collection was assembled by David Riggins
(Texas Department of Commerce, Office of Advanced
Technology, Austin, Texas 78711, 512/320-9561,
david.riggins@tpoint.com).

91

As you'll see from the list below, many of the Gopher Jewels listings tie nicely to the objectives of Goals 2000:

CONTENTS OF GOPHER JEWELS

1. Gopher Jewels Information and Help/
   1. About Gopher Jewels.
   2. Gopher Help Documents/
   3. Gopher Jewels Announcement Archives/
   4. Gopher Jewels Discussion   Archives/
   5. Other Archives and Related Information/

2. Community, Global and Environmental/
   1. Country Specific Information/
   2. Environment/
   3. Free-Nets And Other Community Or State Gophers/
   4. Global or World-Wide Topics/

3. Education, Arts & Humanities/
   1. Anthropology and Archaeology/
   2. Arts and Humanities/
   3. Education (Includes K-12)/
   4. History/
   5. Language/
   6. Religion and Philosophy/
   7. Social Science/

4. Economics, Business and Store Fronts/
   1. Economics and Business/
   2. Products and Services - Store Fronts/

5. Engineering and Industrial Applications/
   1. Architecture/
   2. Engineering Related/
   3. Manufacturing/

6. Government/
   1. Federal Agency and Related Gopher Sites/
   2. Military/
   3. Political and Government/
   4. State Government/

7. Health, Medical, and Disability/
   1. AIDS and HIV Information/
   2. Disability Information/

        3. Medical Related/
        4. Psychology/

8. Internet and Computer Related Resources/
        1. A List Of Gophers With Subject Trees/
        2. Computer Related/
        3. Internet Cyberspace related/
        4. Internet Resources by Type (Gopher, Phone,
USENET, WAIS, Other)/
        5. List of Lists Resources/

9. Law/
        1. Legal or Law related/
        2. Patents and Copyrights/

10. Library, Reference, and News/
        1. Books, Journals, Magazines, Newsletters, and
Publications/
        2. General Reference Resources/
        3. Library Information and Catalogs/
        4. News Related Services/
        5. Radio and TV Broadcasting/

11. Miscellaneous Items/

12. Personal Development and Recreation/
        1. Employment Opportunities and Resume Postings/
        2. Fun Stuff & Multimedia/
        3. Museums, Exhibits and Special Collections/
        4. Travel Information/

13. Physical Sciences including Mathematics/
        1. Agriculture and Forestry/
        2. Astronomy and Astrophysics/
        3. Botany, Biology and Biosciences/
        4. Chemistry/
        5. Geography/
        6. Geology and Oceanography/
        7. Math Sciences/
        8. Meteorology/
        9. Physics/

14. Research, Technology Transfer and Grants
Opportunities/
        1. Grants/
        2. Technical Reports/
        3. Technology Transfer/

The offerings in Gopher Jewels change from time to time as useful new Gopher sites come on line. When you use this tool, you may find a slightly different listing of categories. (Note that the list above shows both the major subject headings and the first level of options under each category.)

With tools like Gopher Jewels and Veronica at your disposal, you are only a few keystrokes away from vast libraries of information and educational resources that you can examine and download from computers located all over the world.

Gems in Gopher Jewels

If you've ever wondered what the weather map looks like for your area, you'll probably find hourly satellite maps for your corner of the world on one of the databases listed under the Gopher Jewels Meteorology category.

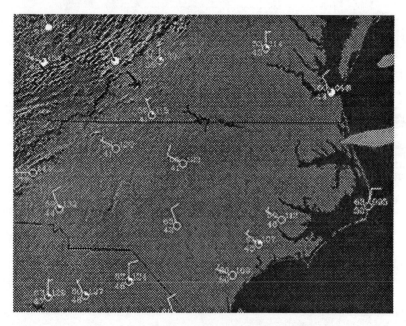

This color map showing part of North Carolina includes composites of visible and infrared (IR) images sent from satellites to computer databases you can reach from the privacy of your own computer.

ftp

Many publicly accessible computer systems support the File Transfer Protocol (ftp). The use of this system is fairly straightforward, especially if you are familiar with operating systems like MS-DOS. Basically, these computers allow you to transfer files to your Internet host, from which you can then download files to the disk drive on your personal computer. This two-step process reflects Net courtesy, since your data transfer from the remote computer takes place (typically) at very high speeds, even if you are using a slow modem from an ordinary telephone line. Once you have transferred a series of files from the remote host to your own Internet provider, you can then download these files to your computer using the file transfer software supported by your terminal program. Since the details of this process vary from system to system, you'll need to explore those details on your own.

To use this system, you need to know which ftp sites are likely to have the material you want transferred. A program called Archie (which operates similarly to Veronica in the Gopher world) will track down ftp sites for you, and you'll also find quite a few sites on your own or by word of mouth. For example, the ftp server at Washington University in St. Louis has a remarkable collection of images of all kinds. To explore (and transfer) images from this site, start the ftp program from your Internet host and enter:

```
open wuarchive.wustl.edu
```

Once you have connected to the remote computer, you will be asked to log in. In general, all you need to do is log in under the name "anonymous" (no quotes, of course). When asked for your password, enter your e-mail address. In my case this would be DThornburg@aol.com. This way the site gets to see who is accessing their files.

Once the login process is completed, you can see a directory of the computer by typing

```
dir
```

The resulting screen contains a lot of material you don't need to decipher. The last column, however, contains the name of subdirectories (or folders) containing more information.

-rw-r--r--	1 root	wheel	792	Mar	13	21:01	
.Links							
-rw-r--r--	1 root	wheel	143	Feb	3	16:29	
.about.html							
-rw-r--r--	1 root	archive	0	Nov	28	1990	
.notar							
drwx------	2 root	wheel	8192	Jan	14	18:36	.tags
-rw-r--r--	1 root	archive	2928	May	17	1993	
README							
-rw-r--r--	1 root	archive	1723	Jun	29	1993	
README.NFS							
d--x--x--x	2 root	wheel	8192	Mar	31	15:44	bin
drwxr-xr-x	9 root	wheel	8192	Apr	28	10:05	decus
drwxr-xr-x	19 root	archive	8192	Feb	7	14:43	doc
drwxr-xr-x	5 root	wheel	8192	Jan	19	17:13	edu
d--x--x--x	7 root	wheel	8192	May	1	02:21	etc
drwxr-xr-x	8 root	wheel	8192	Jan	20	15:27	
graphics							
drwxr-xr-x	4 root	archive	8192	May	11	02:19	info
drwxr-xr-x	8 root	archive	8192	Mar	30	18:46	
languages							
drwxr-xr-x	2 root	wheel	8192	Apr	6	07:46	
mirrors							
drwxr-xr-x	4 root	archive	8192	Jan	15	18:39	
multimedia							
drwxr-xr-x	38 root	archive	8192	May	2	10:07	
packages							
d--x--x--x	3 root	wheel	8192	Mar	8	08:27	
private							
drwxrwxrwx	9 root	wheel	8192	May	10	06:29	pub
drwxr-xr-x	26 root	archive	8192	Apr	17	21:30	
systems							
drwxr-xr-x	35 root	archive	8192	Mar	8	09:20	
usenet							

In our case, we want to examine the contents of the graphics directory, so enter

```
cd graphics
```

and type dir again.

```
-rw-rw-r--   1 root     archive          0 Nov 28  1990
.notar
lrwxr-x---   1 root     wheel           24 Jan 20 15:27
comp.sources.x -> ../usenet/comp.sources.x
lrwxr-xr-x   1 root     wheel           24 Jan 20 06:49 gif
-> ../multimedia/images/gif
lrwxr-x---   1 root     wheel           29 Jan 20 15:27 gif-
news -> ../multimedia
/images/gif-news
drwxr-xr-x  19 archiver archive       8192 May  8 11:11
graphics
drwxr-xr-x   2 root     wheel         8192 Jan 19 18:48
lpr_art
drwxr-xr-x   2 root     wheel         8192 Jan 19 19:02
magellan
drwxr-xr-x   2 root     wheel         8192 Jan 19 18:56
radiology
drwxr-xr-x  10 pullen   archive       8192 Apr  9 13:43
trains
drwxrwxrwx   3 x313     archive       8192 Jan 25 08:16 x313
```

Looking at this list, I noticed "gif". GIF files are image files
that have been compressed — a good sign! By changing to this
directory and listing the result, you'll find a long list of entries
(part of which is shown below).

```
.
.
.
drwxr-xr-x   2 archiver archive       8192 Jan 20 15:50 k
drwxr-xr-x   2 archiver archive       8192 Jan 20 15:53 l
drwxr-xr-x   2 archiver archive       8192 Jan 20 15:55 m
drwxr-xr-x   2 archiver archive       8192 Jan 20 15:58 n
.
.
.
```

Each of these directories contains the image files themselves.
For example, if you want a copy of the Mona Lisa, you might

look under the "m" directory. Sure enough, there it is along with hundreds of other pictures starting with "m".

.
.
.

```
-rw-rw-r--  1 archiver archive   43436 Oct 30  1989
moines.gif
- 383468 Aug 16  1992 mona.gif
-rw-r--r--  1 archiver archive  172066 Aug 17  1992
monaco1.gif
-rw-rw-r--  1 archiver archive  161512 Oct 30  1989
monalisa.gif
-rw-rw-r--  1 archiver archive   18507 Oct 30  1989
monalisa2.gif
-rw-r--r--  1 archiver archive   17792 Feb 10  1993
monatw.gif
-rw-rw-r--  1 archiver archive   49152 Jan 11  1991
monika.gif
```

.
.
.

When you find a file you want copied, type

```
get filename
```

where filename is the name of the file you want transferred EXACTLY as it appears in the list. Every punctuation mark and capitalization is meaningful, so be careful! In other words,

```
get monalisa.gif
```

will transfer the file to your host computer, and

```
get Mona Lisa.gif
```

will not!

Once you have a set of files transferred to your Internet host, type "bye" to leave the ftp session and return to your host. At that point, choose the "download" option to bring your files onto the disk drive in your personal computer.

This process is more cumbersome than using gophers, and many ftp sites support gophers as well; but for those that don't, ftp is an invaluable resource! And, as you can see, your very own copy of the Mona Lisa is there for you to edit or use as you wish!

Listservs and Newsgroups

The other resources loaded with relevant information on many of the education goals are "listservs" and "Usenet newsgroups". A listserv is basically a mailing list to which you subscribe.

Subscriptions are started by sending an e-mail message to the "listserv" address requesting that your mailbox be added to the distribution list. In general, the process looks like this:

To subscribe to a discussion group:
1. Send e-mail message to the listserv address
2. Leave the subject line blank
3. In the text type: Subscribe GROUP Your name

4. Send the message

(GROUP should be replaced with the name of the listserv discussion group you want to join. After that, type your first and last name.)

Items forwarded to that list by any member are automatically sent to your mailbox (e-mail or electronic mail provided as part of your basic service). By signing up for listservs in your interest area, you become part of a huge global community of like-minded people who can share ideas, questions, and resources with each other. Unlike normal (paper) mail, your messages are sent immediately. If you ask a question, you are likely to start getting responses within a few minutes. The only risk with listservs is that the volume of mail you get may be enormous. I'm very choosy about the listservs to which I belong, and I still get about forty messages a day.

An alternative (and mostly) non-overlapping way to maintain ongoing dialogues on topics of interest to you is to subscribe to one or more "Usenet newsgroups" germane to your areas of interest.

Technically, Usenet messages are shipped around the world, from host system to host system, using one of several specific Net protocols. Your host system stores all of its Usenet messages in one place, which everybody with an account on the system can access. That way, no matter how many people actually read a given message, each host system has to store only one copy of it.

Usenet is huge. Every day, Usenet users pump upwards of 25 million characters into the system — roughly the equivalent of volumes A-E of the Encyclopedia Britannica.

The basic building block of Usenet is the newsgroup, which is a collection of messages with a related theme (on other networks, these would be called conferences, forums, bulletin boards or special-interest groups). There are now about 5,000 of these newsgroups, many related to issues connected with Goals 2000.

New education-related groups are added all the time. The Gopher server at the University of Michigan keeps lists of education-related newsgroups and listservs. These lists are large (hundreds of pages), but contain some real gems! Without question, you'll find groups related to each of the eight goals.

Pictures in the Text

Newsgroups contain text files only, so to send images, sounds and movies over the Net, they must be converted to text files first using special software. (This process is called UUEncoding, and the UULite program on the CD-ROM will both encode and decode files for you.)

This picture of Laurel and Hardy was downloaded as a text file. A portion of the text encoding the picture is shown below:

```
begin 0666 laurhard.jpg
M_]C_X  02D9)1@ !  $  $  $  R #(  #__@  #__@ 752U,96%D(%-Y<W1E;;7,L
M_]L OP  (!08'!08(!P<)"08("0P*"@H*#@T-#@X+#@X+#@X"00P&!@8&!@8&!@8&
M*R(;*R(+,3$Y&&+K>(,&&J@L-,0L-,L01$,LM9BU-JQ6M-,NS]DNMT+D<&R[;O!K;
M  $  " "  TM" #@<G'0!" "  $7W"@Q

M(G$J+KJUURy5  $  " "
M1TA)1)4@$?3IGyJ5JNFKY4s"*I
M1234  567890%E:8V1E9F=H:zzza5=WAY]H'0v=WAY>H.$_A8:'B(F*D.4E
MHJ.D::GJ+yes.TM;;WN+FPZPT/$Q;rs;'R':G*V
```

(Pretty cryptic, eh?)

Some Thoughts...

It is not uncommon for new users to feel overwhelmed, as if they are trying to get a drink of water from a fire hydrant. The key, I think, is to realize that these tools aren't going away; you don't have to find everything today. Pick and choose your way through a subject area to get the feel of the Net, and enjoy your wanderings. Watch out, though, for you may find that you've been on the Net for several hours, even if it only feels like a few minutes! Unlimited access to information in an area that engages you is enticing.

Details on the use of gophers, listservs and newsgroups are beyond the scope of this document. There are a lot of great books on the topic, however, and your local library or bookstore will be more than happy to assist you in your selection. One good starting book (available over the Internet and through some commercial services like America Online) is the *Big Dummy's Guide to the Internet* written by Adam Gaffin as a result of conversations between Mitch Kapor (of the Electronic Frontier Foundation) and Steve Cisler (of Apple Computer). This book was intentionally placed on a variety of networks to make it easy to get. (Use Veronica to search for Big Dummy and see what you get!) Of course, if you don't want to download a version from the Net, you could always read the copy we've enclosed on the CD-ROM.

What If I Make a Mistake?

Mistakes happen every day. It takes time to learn anything new — and this is especially true for navigating the Net. The Internet was not designed with non-technical users in mind. You'll sometimes end up in strange places, or find a cryptic message on your screen that you don't understand. You may even have your computer come screeching to a halt. If that happens, just turn off your modem, turn off your computer, and start over again. Don't worry about breaking the Internet — it can't be done. The Internet was designed to withstand all-out nuclear attack. Yes, you'll get frustrated, and yes, you'll make mistakes, but the rewards are well worth the effort you'll be putting into mastering this new tool.

One final comment is in order before you start using newsgroups or subscribe to listservs: "lurk" for awhile before adding your thoughts to the discussion. Many of these groups have been active for a long time, and discussion threads should be honored before you add your ideas or questions to the discussion.

Also, and this is VERY important, the world of listservs and newsgroups is littered with opinions from many points of view. Don't accept everything you read as true. The Net mimics real life in this respect — check your sources and keep your mind alert at all times.

Now we'll link the eight goals to Internet resources. Once again, know that the Net is growing at a phenomenal rate and, by the time you read this, many more resources will be available. Our goal is not to stuff you with information, but to provide a taste for the rich resources available to you as you work to achieve these goals.

Goal 1: All children in America will start school ready to learn.

This goal addresses a broad range of topics including pre-natal care, nutrition, and other factors influencing children's readiness to learn. This area is the topic of several listservs and other resources. Here are a few to get you started:

```
ECENET-L     LISTSERV@UIUCVMD.BITNET    Early childhood
education/young children (0-8)
ECEOL-L      LISTSERV@MAINE.BITNET      Early Childhood
Education On-Line mailing list
```

A brief search on ERIC showed seventeen articles on school readiness.

Goal 2: The high school graduation rate will increase to at least 90 percent.

If we are truly going to provide a quality education for all students, and have them succeed, we need to insure that their special needs are addressed. This includes attentiveness to differences in learning styles among students, as well as other factors relating to cultural issues and any identified special needs that students might have. Special needs must be addressed for all students — those who are gifted as well as those who have difficulty with traditional school work. The needs of those who are kinesthetically gifted and interested in high-skills work in areas not requiring a four-year college degree must be addressed as well, since only 26% of our youth currently graduate from college.

This area is the topic of several listservs and other resources. Here are a few to get you started:

```
giftednet-1 listserver@listserv.cc.wm.edu  Gifted Education
MULTC-ED      LISTSERV@UMDD.BITNET Multicultural Education
Discussion
NAT-EDU       LISTSERV@MIAMIU.BITNET      Educational needs
of indigenous peoples
spedtalk      MAJORDOMO@VIRGINIA.EDU      Discussion of
Topics in Special Education
TAG-L         LISTSERV@NDSUVM1.BITNET     Talented and
Gifted Education
UCVE-L        LISTSERV@OSUVM1.BITNET      UCVE-L Vocational
Teacher Education Task Force
```

A search of the ERIC database uncovered fifty-seven articles related to dropout prevention.

Goal 3: All students will leave grades 4, 8, and 12 having demonstrated competency over challenging subject matter including English, mathematics, science, foreign languages, civics and government, economics, the arts, history, and geography, and every school in America will ensure that all students learn to use their minds well, so they may be prepared for responsible citizenship, further learning, and productive employment in our nation's modern economy.

First, let's explore resources that assist in the demonstration of competency and thinking skills.

Expression of mastery can take many forms. In addition to the traditional written report, students can take advantage of multimedia tools to express their knowledge in ways that incorporate text, graphics, animation, sound, and computer models. The flexibility of the computer medium is especially important for students whose learning and expressive styles are broader than those of the purely linguistic learner. Howard Gardner's research at Harvard has shown that each of us has at least seven distinct intelligences through which we develop and express our understanding of any subject. The traditional term paper address one or two of these. Multimedia expresses many more.

Fortunately, the resources on the Internet are already in a form that multimedia authoring tools can use. While numerous commercial multimedia tools are available, there are many tools in the public domain or in shareware libraries that can be used by students and teachers alike for the creation of disk-based (as opposed to paper-based) documents. Disk-based documents can incorporate text, sounds, color images and movies quite easily. To name just one example, DOCMaker for the Macintosh is very easy to use, and supports a variety of media with a fraction of the effort required to master most word processors.

Software libraries that contain multimedia authoring tools accessible through ftp or gopher can be found many places on the Net. Reviews of popular public-domain and shareware programs can often be found in trade magazines (or in newsgroups).

Literally thousands of programs are available for downloading from the Net. To get a sense of the vastness of the public-domain and shareware collections available, use Veronica to search on the phrase "Macintosh software" or "Windows software". When I did this recently, I uncovered over one hundred sites with collections of software for the Mac, and over forty with extensive collections of Windows and MS-DOS software. The challenge is not in finding software collections, but in locating high quality products that meet your needs. This is where published reviews and user's groups come in handy!

In addition to the vast subject matter libraries you can access through tools like Gopher Jewels, there are numerous newsgroups devoted to the content areas relevant to Goals 2000. A brief list of some groups (along with their listserv addresses) is provided below:

```
BUGNET       LISTSERV@WSUVM1.BITNET      Insect Education
BUSED-L      LISTSERV@UREGINA1.BITNET    A Forum for
Discussion of Business Education
CBEHIGH      LISTSERV@BLEKUL11.BITNET    Computers in
education
CHEMED-L     LISTSERV@UWF.BITNET    Chemistry Education
Discussion List
CIPE-L       LISTSERV@UWF.BITNET    Computers in Physics
Education
IMSE-L       LISTSERV@UICVM.BITNET       Institute for Math
and Science Education
JOURNET      LISTSERV@QUCDN.BITNET       Discussion List
for Journalism Education
PhotoForum   listserv@listserver.isc.rit.edu
        Photo/Imaging Education List
JTE-L        LISTSERV@VTVM1.CC.VT.EDU     Journal of
Technology Education
MATHEDCC     LISTSERV@MCGILL1.BITNET     The Technology in
Mathematics Education forum
NCPRSE-L     LISTSERV@ECUVM1.BITNET      Reform discussion
list for Science Education
```

Caveat: The vast resources of the Internet provide so much content that the unwary educator might be falsely impressed by voluminous tomes handed in by students who have successfully downloaded large quantities of information. Our goal is not to just find the relevant information, but to make meaning from it — to demonstrate understanding of challenging material in each of the subject matter domains. The acquisition of raw information is an important first step in the process, but it is the application of this information that truly matters in the long run.

Goal 4: The Nation's teaching force will have access to programs for the continued improvement of their professional skills and the opportunity to acquire the knowledge and skills needed to instruct and prepare all American students for the next century.

As educators, we need resources to help us reinvent our craft in ways that help students prepare themselves for a future quite different from our past. Teaching is very demanding and exhausting. Many educators feel like voices in the wilderness, unsure how to reach out for assistance when they want it. Educators need resources to help them understand the new technologies that provide additional resources to them. Some listservs that explore these topics are shown below:

```
BGEDU-L      LISTSERV@UKCC.BITNET  BGEDU-L is a forum for
the quality of education
EDNET        listserv@nic.umass.edu      Use of networks in
education
EDPOLYAN     LISTSERV@ASUACAD.BITNET     Professionals and
Students Discussing Education
EDPOLYAR     LISTSERV@ASUACAD.BITNET     Education Policy
Analysis Archives: An Electronic Journal
EDTECH       LISTSERV@MSU.BITNET   EDTECH - Educational
Technology
EDTECPOL     LISTSERV@UMDD.BITNET  Conference on Educational
Technology Policy
EDUTEL       LISTSERV@RPIECS.BITNET      Education and
information technologies
ERL-L        LISTSERV@ASUACAD.BITNET     Educational
Research List
EUITLIST     LISTSERV@BITNIC.BITNET      Educational Uses
of Information Technology
FORSUM-L     LISTSERV@BROWNVM.BITNET     Educational
Institution Networks
JESSE        LISTSERV@ARIZVM1.BITNET     Open
Library/Information Science Education Forum
MEDIA-L      LISTSERV@BINGVMB.BITNET   Media in Education
NEWEDU-L     LISTSERV@USCVM.BITNET     New Paradigms in
Education List
```

```
NREN-Discuss        nren-discuss-request@psi.com
      National Research Education Network
SS435-L      LISTSERV@UALTAVM.BITNET       Elementary teacher
education list
TERSG-L      LISTSERV@UBVM.BITNET NRC: Teacher Education
Research Study Group
ucp-acl      ucp-acl@mit.edu       Educational Priorities
UKERA-L      LISTSERV@UKCC.BITNET Dialogue on Educational
Reform
```

ERIC's database contains numerous articles on pedagogy, restructuring, and other topics of ongoing interest to educators.

Goal 5: United States students will be first in the world in mathematics and science achievement.

This area is receiving a great deal of attention on the Internet, and in Washington. One of the major recent programs related to this topic is the GLOBE (Global Learning and Observations to Benefit the Environment) Program initiated by Vice President Gore.

In this program, school children, educators and scientists worldwide will work together to study the global environment.

The objectives of the GLOBE Program are:
- to enhance the collective awareness of individuals throughout the world concerning the environment,
- to increase scientific understanding of the Earth, and
- to help all students reach higher standards in science and mathematics education.

The GLOBE Program consists of a worldwide network of K-12 Students:
- making environmental observations at or near their school (e.g., measurement of air temperature, wind speed and direction, precipitation, land cover, water chemistry and soil moisture content),
- providing data useful to environmental scientists, and
- sharing the resulting global environmental images and knowledge with each other.

The GLOBE Program will employ an international information network, initially using the Internet, direct satellite transmission and television. The network will support:
- the acquisition of environmental data by students,
- transmission of the data to processing sites in the U.S. and other countries,
- distribution of vivid, graphical environmental pictures of the world to students at their schools, and
- distribution of student data to environmental scientists throughout the world.

Scientists are involved in the design and implementation of the GLOBE program and will help determine what types of measurements students are most capable of making and where students can make the greatest contribution.

The data acquired by the students are expected to be useful in the understanding of earth systems by students and environmental researchers in a wide range of fields. The student data will be quality-controlled during GLOBE processing prior to their use in producing environmental images and publicly available data.

It is the goal of the GLOBE Program to have over 200 schools participate in initial GLOBE implementation by April 22, 1995, the 25th Earth Day. Over the following few years, the program will grow with hundreds more schools becoming actively involved. Over 60 countries have expressed interest in participating.

You can keep up with this project through their Gopher site, globe.gov.

The Gopher Jewels collection is a great place for browsers interested in math and science resources. If you have a specific subject you want to explore, Veronica is a good bet. Just enter the subject you're interested in, and let your computer track it down for you!

In addition to gopher and ftp sites, there are many education-related listservs that can help you as well. Some of these are listed below:

```
IAMS iams-request@quack.kfu.com   Internet Amateur
Mathematics Society
IMSE-L       LISTSERV@UICVM.BITNET        Institute for Math
and Science Education
JCMST-L      LISTSERV@PURCCVM.BITNET      Journal of
Computers in Mathematics and Science
MATHEDCC     LISTSERV@MCGILL1.BITNET      The Technology in
Mathematics Education (TiME)
mathgroup    mathgroup-request@yoda.ncsa.uiuc.edu
     Mathmatica
mathmagic-10-12    majordomo@forum.swarthmore.edu      10-
12 Math Problem Solving Skills
mathmagic-10-12-open      majordomo@forum.swarthmore.edu
     10-12 Math Problem Solving Skills
mathmagic-4-6      majordomo@forum.swarthmore.edu      4-6
Math Problem Solving Skills
mathmagic-4-6-open majordomo@forum.swarthmore.edu      4-6
Math Problem Solving Skills
mathmagic-7-9      majordomo@forum.swarthmore.edu      7-9
Math Problem Solving Skills
mathmagic-7-9-open majordomo@forum.swarthmore.edu      7-9
Math Problem Solving Skills
mathmagic-general-open    majordomo@forum.swarthmore.edu
     10-12 Math Problem Solving Skills
mathmagic-k-3      majordomo@forum.swarthmore.edu      K-3
Math Problem Solving Skills
mathmagic-k-3-open majordomo@forum.swarthmore.edu      K-3
Math Problem Solving Skills
MSPROJ       LISTSERV@MSU.BITNET   Annenberg/CPB Math &
Science Project
MSUPBND      LISTSERV@UBVM.BITNET  Math Science Upward Bound
Discussion List
NCTM-L       listproc@sci-ed.fit.edu        Teachers of
Mathmatics
AAASMSP      LISTSERV@GWUVM.BITNET        AAAS Minority
Perspectives on Ethics in Science
ANSSTDS      LISTSERV@MSU.BITNET   Animal Science
ASCD-SCI     LISTSERV@PSUVM.BITNET        Alliance for
Teaching of Science
ASIS-L       LISTSERV@UVMVM.BITNET        ASIS-L: American
Society for Information Sciences
ASLIST-L     LISTSERV@VTVM1.BITNET        Arts and Sciences
INFORMATION LIST
```

```
CURDEV-L      LISTSERV@PSUORVM.BITNET       CURDEV-L Science
Curriculum Development List
DARWIN-L      listserv@ukanaix.cc.ukans.edu       Historical
Sciences
DISTLABS      LISTSERV@MIAMIU.BITNET       Teaching Science
Labs Via Distance
FAMLYSCI      LISTSERV@UKCC.BITNET  Family Science Network
FIST  FIST-request@hamp.hampshire.edu      Feminism in/and
Science and Technology
HOPOS-L       LISTSERV@UKCC.BITNET  History of Philosophy of
Science
HPSST-L       LISTSERV@QUCDN.BITNET        History and
Philosophy of Science
IMSE-L        LISTSERV@UICVM.BITNET        Institute for Math
and Science Education
MEDSCI-L      LISTSERV@BROWNVM.BITNET       Medieval and
Renaissance science
MSPROJ        LISTSERV@MSU.BITNET  Annenberg/CPB Math &
Science Project
MSUPBND       LISTSERV@UBVM.BITNET  Math Science Upward Bound
Discussion List
NATOSCI@BLEKUL11.BITNET       LISTSERV@BLEKUL11.BITNET
     Information on the NATO Science and Environment
NATOSCI@CC1.KULEUVEN.AC.BE LISTSERV@CC1.KULEUVEN.AC.BE  NATO
Science Programme
NCPRSE-L      LISTSERV@ECUVM1.BITNET       Reform discussion
list for Science Education
REGSC-L       LISTSERV@WVNVM.BITNET        Regional Science
Information Exchange
SAIS-L        LISTSERV@UNB.ca      Science Awareness and
Promotion
T321-L        LISTSERV@MIZZOU1.BITNET       Teaching Science
in Elementary Schools
```

Goal 6: Every adult American will be literate and will possess the knowledge and skills necessary to compete in a global economy and exercise the rights and responsibilities of citizenship.

Adult literacy and education is increasingly important in a world in which there are few jobs for low-skilled workers, and when future workers will undergo numerous career changes in their lifetimes. The educational needs of today's adults must be addressed along with those of our children. Distance education is especially important for adult learners since they are typically holding down full-time jobs and may need to schedule added educational opportunities into evening time home-based studies. Some listservs that address related issues are shown below:

```
CREAD       LISTSERV@YORKVM1.BITNET    Electronic Network
for Distance Education
ASAT-EVA    LISTSERV@UNLVM.BITNET      AG-SAT Distance
Education Evaluation Group
DED-L       LISTSERV@UALTAVM.BITNET    Distance Education
DEOS-L      LISTSERV@PSUVM.BITNET      DEOSNEWS - The
Distance Education Online Symposium
HMEDRSCH    LISTSERV@ETSUADMN.BITNET   Home Education
Research Discussion List
home-ed     home-ed@think.com      Home Education
NCEOA-L     LISTSERV@NDSUVM1.BITNET    National Council
of Educational Opportunity
NBEA-L      LISTSERV@AKRONVM.BITNET    National Business
Education Association Discussion
TESLIT-L    LISTSERV@CUNYVM.BITNET     TESLIT-L: Adult
Education and Literacy
WVUPFF-L    LISTSERV@WVNVM.BITNET      Adult
Education/Distance Learning Discussion
```

Goal 7: Every school in the United States will be free of drugs, violence, and the unauthorized presence of firearms and alcohol and will offer a disciplined environment conducive to learning.

One listserv related to this topic is:

```
DRUGABUS    LISTSERV@UMAB.BITNET  Drug Abuse Education
Information and Research
```

Other resources can be found through the numerous government databases and file servers. ERIC, for example, has well over a hundred articles relating to drug abuse, school violence, and safety-related issues.

Goal 8: Every school will promote partnerships that will increase parental involvement and participation

in promoting the social, emotional, and academic growth of children.

ERIC's database contains over fourteen articles on parenting, and references to numerous other resources of value to parents.

Parental involvement is a major component of school success. One of the beauties of having informational technologies at home is that parents can use the same telecomputing resources to enhance their own skills that their children are using. Children model what they see at home. If parents are active learners themselves, their children are likely to maintain their enthusiasm for learning as well.

Unlike passive activities like watching television, navigating the Net is, by its nature, highly interactive. A search that starts down one path quickly branches into a multiplicity of choices that can form the basis of a knowledge adventure for entire families. Because these adventures can take place in homes or libraries where Net access is available, parents and children can develop close connections around the topic of lifelong learning. Toward that end, I would hope that parents feel encouraged to explore any and all of the resources listed above.

Technology Planning for the Communication Age

A Technology Planning Template with Focus Questions

If you don't have a destination, then any route will get you there.

— *Anonymous*

Introduction to the Template:

This document provides a framework for the creation of a technology plan for educational institutions based on the recent shift from the era of information to that of communications. This template contains background material, focus questions, and some reference documents to help you shape your own technology plan. As this document represents certain pedagogical biases of the author, you should edit the plan to reflect the underlying beliefs of your own organization.

Using the Template:

First, provide copies of this chapter to every member of your planning team and have them develop new questions and possible answers to the questions we've included to guide your thinking. (I've placed a DOCMaker version of this chapter on the CD-ROM for you to give out or print for all members of the planning team.)

You might want to schedule several meetings to brainstorm on the ideas raised in this document, and to add your new ideas to the plan. Above all, don't feel restricted by any of the ideas or questions I've raised. You are in the best position to know what the needs are in your community, so trust the expertise in your own home base!

Once you are ready to draft your own document, you can start with this one as a template. Choose Save Text from the Export option in the File menu to create a text file you can then edit with your own word processor or page layout program. Replace the questions we've raised with their answers, create a budget, and you'll be well on the way to having a technology plan designed to meet the needs of your school or district as we prepare for the next century.

I: Underlying Concepts

Educational technology should be used to serve an instructional paradigm needed to prepare students for life in the 21st century. In the past few years we have experienced some "reversals" that shape some of the trends likely to be important for the remainder of the century. A few of these trends are listed below:

- The downsizing of large corporations and the rise of the sole practitioner or small organization: Fortune 500 companies have downsized 25% in the last 20 years, and over 50% of all new companies have only one employee.

- The death of the Information Age and the emergence of the Communication Age: IBM, anxious to recover from a multi-billion dollar loss, is shifting away from mainframes and into communications technologies. Communication industry mergers and the "information superhighway" are daily newspaper topics.

- High-skill workers continue to see their wages and job opportunities increase, while low-skill workers see their wages and jobs disappear: Re-employment and school-to-work educational programs are being designed to insure that everyone has the lifelong educational opportunities needed to acquire the high level of skills needed to thrive in the coming years.

These changes (and many others) are driving the reinvention of America's schools. The educational system of the past is being redesigned to meet the needs of a world that has changed considerably in the past few decades.

Technology has a large role to play in the reinvention of schools, but the implementation of computers, instructional video, and telecommunication links will be meaningless unless they are designed into a curriculum and are chosen to support pedagogical models designed to insure the maximum learning opportunities for all students. Technology, alone, cannot drive reform. If technology is brought into classrooms without revisiting the curricular and pedagogical issues, it risks being used to implement the educational strategies of the past. We will, in effect, have placed a gas engine in a horse, rather than designed an automobile.

This is an important point, one worth stressing. Curriculum and pedagogy must drive technology use. Technology implemented in the absence of a broader plan almost always leads to disaster. One advantage that comes from placing technology in its proper perspective is that technology purchases will have long-term value in the face of constant price/performance improvements. When technology is purchased to meet specific curricular or pedagogical goals, it will continue to meet these objectives when newer technology comes out. On the other hand, technology purchased just because it is the "latest thing" will lose its value the instant the next new technology hits the streets.

It is impossible to keep up with the latest and greatest technological wonders, even if technology budgets are enormous. It is important to insure that technology is purchased to meet a clearly identified opportunity for learning, not just to bring "high tech" into a facility.

Curricular Reform Focus Questions:
If your state has new educational frameworks, this is the time to review those frameworks and think about the role that

technology can play in the implementation of a new curriculum. If you are implementing national guidelines (NCTM, etc.) these should be reviewed as well. Enter your responses to these questions below:

- How can technology help in exposing learners to new concepts and ideas in the curricular areas?

- How can technology help learners acquire up-to-date information on the subjects they are studying?

- How can technology help learners work collaboratively with peers both at their local site and world-wide in their pursuit of a topic?

- How can technology be used to help students create interactive multimedia projects that serve as assessment vehicles for their studies?

Pedagogical Focus Questions:

If you are shifting educational strategies to provide improved learning opportunities for all students, review these in the context of the following questions and enter your responses below: (These questions assume an instructional model that accommodates different learning styles, e.g., Gardner's theory of multiple intelligences.)

- What technologies are most appropriate for the variety of learning styles found in your classrooms?

- What types of presentation tools are needed to insure that the needs of the visual, auditory and kinesthetic learners are met?

- What types of technology tools should be accessible by individual students so they can explore subjects in ways that are natural to them?

II: Access

The walls of the classroom must be open to access through a variety of telecommunication services. Most students' homes have telephones and access to cable television. Most classrooms do not. In the 19th century homes were less likely to have access to information than classrooms. Today it is the classrooms that are challenged.

This plan addresses these issues as follows:

Communication Access Focus Questions:
- What is the current status of CATV (cable television) to each of your classrooms? What plans do you have to expand this service if needed?

- What type of satellite services do you have on your campus? What plans do you have to increase your access to satellite communication? Do you plan to explore the new direct broadcast satellite services (DirecTV by RCA)?

- What is the current status of outside phone lines to each of your classrooms? What plans do you have to expand this service if needed? Rather than bring phone lines to each classroom, do you plan to add a "telephone server" as part of a local area network (LAN), or do you plan to install a multiline PBX system with access to each classroom?

- What is the current status of your campus-wide local area network (LAN)? Is it connected to other services (e.g., an Internet host)? Do you have high-speed network connections to each classroom? What plans do you have to add capacity if needed?

- What is the current status of ISDN (Integrated Services Digital Network) lines on your campus? Is your local telephone company offering special ISDN services for educational institutions? Do these services afford you new educational opportunities that justify bringing these services to your classrooms?

- If you are in California, have you taken advantage of the Education First initiative through which PacBell provides up to four ISDN lines per school site in its service area with no installation charge, and no service fee for the first year? (1-800-901-2210)

- Does your campus have its own Internet host? Do you intend to secure a high-speed connection to the Internet, or to a local university of college (or other organization) where such a service might be provided? While you might have low-speed (14.4 kb/sec) connections to the Internet over analog phone lines from each classroom, is there one dedicated high-speed digital connection available on campus? Is this connection in the school library or other place providing easy access to students and faculty alike?

- What dial-up connections are available for students to use at home when they want to connect to the school network, or to gain access to the Internet?

III: Destinations

Telecommunication pathways and on-ramps are meaningless without interesting destinations. In order to support the needs of all learners and educators, this technology plan brings all members of our learning community into contact with vast libraries of information, and into contact with their peers wherever in the world they might be.

In the Middle Ages, information was treated as a scarce resource, and the role of teachers was to disseminate and parcel this information out to the community of learners in their midst. The role of educator as content expert has been defined and refined through the years.

But today's reality transforms the role of educator to that of the Latin root: *educare* — to lead or draw out. Rather than function primarily as a source of information, today's educators become co-learners or field guides in the exploration of content. The content itself is accessible through numerous sources. The community library with 110,000 titles pales in comparison to the vast libraries of information that are available to anyone with an account on the Internet or commercial information service.

The reversal in the educator's role from information deliverer to field guide requires extensive staff development (to be addressed later in this plan). It also requires access to informational destinations. Numerous services are available today, and many more are being added daily. The Internet is adding about 230 new hosts per hour, 24-hours a day, 365 days a year.

Communication Service Focus Questions:

- Do you subscribe to *Cable in the Classroom* magazine (1-800-216-2225) to receive monthly download schedules of educational television programming from A&E, BET, Bravo, CNBC, C-SPAN and 19 other television channels? (Note: Your local cable provider should be arranging for a free subscription to this magazine.)

- Do you have access to X•Press X•Change in your classrooms? This service provides numerous real-time wire feeds from newswires all over the planet (AP, Tass, National Weather Service, CNN, etc.) and is often offered free to schools by your local cable provider. X•Press X•Change uses a special modem to connect your television cable to a computer for the newswire feeds. The received information is then saved on your disk. For information on this service call: 1-800-7PC-NEWS.

- Do you have access to one or more commercial services such as America Online, Prodigy, Genie, Compuserve, etc.? Have teachers been made aware of any special discounts for these services that might be available to them? (America Online, for example, provides deep discounts to NEA members.)

- Does your state provide access to the Internet for educators through its own educational network? Many states have special educational networks for use by educators. If your state has this capability, do all educators know how to get their own accounts and use the variety of services provided?

- Does your local PBS affiliate offer accounts on Learning Link to educators? If so, are educators in your school or district connected to this service?

- Does your site have its own high speed Internet node? Have you explored the possibility of securing a dedicated broadband connection to the Internet (probably located in a library or other place of easy general access)?

While online services are invaluable for correspondence (e-mail) and current information, CD-ROM's are likely to be more cost effective distribution vehicles for archival information for the next few years. For this reason, CD-ROM access is as important as access to online services. This is why every computer purchased under this plan should have a built-in CD-ROM drive.

CD-ROM Software Focus Questions:
- Do you currently subscribe to the *Nautilus* CD-ROM? This monthly publication, available for both the Macintosh and Windows platforms, provides a rich array of materials relating to education, industry news, desktop media, entertainment, software tools, and public-domain software and shareware (1-800-637-3472).

- Have you started a library of NASA image CD-ROM's from the numerous missions to various parts of the solar system? (National Space Science Data Center, Goddard Space Flight Center, Greenbelt, MD 20771. 301-286-6695)

- Do you subscribe to *CD-ROM Professional*, *New Media*, *Morph's Outpost*, and other journals devoted to keeping you updated on new software being published on CD-ROM's?

- Do you have the latest *Library of the Future* CD-ROM containing about a thousand classical works of literature, or do you have other literary compilations available on CD-ROM?

IV. Equipment and Software

This technology plan is based on the idea that curriculum and pedagogy should drive software selection, and that software should drive hardware acquisition. Today the two common platforms for educational computing are the Macintosh and IBM compatible machines. The recent entry of PowerPC-based computers offers, for the first time, true cross-platform compatibility along with the capacity to run new programs with pronounced improvement in speed and performance over versions designed for either of the native (Macintosh or PC) platforms.

There are other computer platforms of interest to educators for special applications. For example, the Amiga may be an excellent choice for traditional video production since it is designed specifically for compatibility with the U. S. television NTSC standard for color displays. The popularity of the Video Toaster software/hardware add-ons for this platform increases its utility in this domain, making the Amiga an excellent choice for either broadcast of videotape production. (At the time of this writing, Commodore is in the process of reorganization, so the Amiga may find a different and more congenial home.)

Higher-end workstation platforms (such as those from Sun and Silicon Graphics) have their place as well, especially in the realm of network hosts, servers and high-resolution color graphics. In the next few years we will see a battle waged in the higher end of the personal computer platform market as companies like Silicon Graphics lower the prices of their offerings while Apple increases the capability of its product line.

These points aside, technology purchases need to be driven by software, and for education (especially in the K-12 world) the bulk of equipment purchases for the classroom will be split between the Apple Macintosh (or PowerPC) platform and the IBM-compatible machines.

This plan recognizes that computer prices are dropping while performance improves, and that any purchase made today will be out of date in three months. It is also the case, however, that every day's delay in securing the hardware and software needed for education steals precious time from the educators and students who will benefit from these tools. Accordingly, technology purchases are made with the anticipation of a useful equipment life of five years or less.

Computer hardware specifications

Every desk-based computer system should have at least the following: (Note that these are minimum specifications.)

- Color monitor with 256 colors at a resolution of 640x480 pixels.

- Built-in hard disk with at least 80 MB capacity (Macintosh) or larger (for Windows) for application and system software storage.

- Built-in CD-ROM drive (triple or quad speed multi-session mechanism designed to meet the CD-ROM XA protocols).

- Built-in local area network support (based on the capabilities of your LAN).

- High speed modem (14.4 kb/sec) if online services are provided through ordinary phone lines.

- Large capacity removable media storage device for multimedia projects. (Computer images and sound files are typically quite large. While these files can be efficiently compressed once the project is completed, they should be left in their uncompressed state during editing. It is common for a work in progress to require a very large amount of disk space during creation, yet end up on a single high-density floppy disk when completed.)

This external storage system could be a high speed drive based on the Syquest or Bernoulli technologies, or less expensive, but slower, magneto-optical drives such as the 128 Mbyte MO drives currently offered by many vendors. The Sony Minidisc technology will emerge soon, and this should be added to the possible list of choices. Note that the high speed magnetic media (e.g., Syquest) typically cost twice as much per megabyte as the magneto-optical media.

- Sound capture capability of at least 22 kHz at 8-bits with the option of expansion to 44 kHz at 16-bits (CD quality audio) if needed.

- Analog video capture capability allowing images from student-generated video tapes to be captured as either still images or movies. Still image capture should support full-screen 8-bit (256 colors) or higher resolution.

Additional Peripheral Hardware Includes:

- High-resolution color projection system to show computer images on a screen. This can consist of either a video projector or a liquid crystal color display plate used in conjunction with a high-brightness (5,500 lumens or more) overhead projector.

- High resolution color scanner for flat art (600 dpi or more) for digitizing color photographs or other images that might be already available on paper.

- Digital still camera for capturing color still images that can be transferred directly to the computer without needing any extra equipment for image conversion (Apple QuickTake 100, for example.)

- Copystand type document camera for capturing images of small objects.

- Video Camcorder.

- NTSC scan converter to allow computer images to be mixed with video images and/or recorded on videotape (e.g., the TelevEyes device from Digital Vision.)

- Portable keyboard with data storage capability (e.g., the AlphaSmart keyboard for the Macintosh.)

- Sound system for stereo playback of multimedia sounds.

- MIDI music synthesizer.

- Laser videodisc player with computer interface (e.g., Pioneer 2400).

- Do you plan to provide point-to-point video services over ISDN lines? If so, are you planning to install special video equipment such as that provided by Compression Labs, or use special software/hardware enhancements on desktop computers? (Cornell University's CU-SeeMe software is free and is enclosed on the CD-ROM.)

- What additional requirements do you have?

Software Specifications:
- Integrated "works" software incorporating word processor, spreadsheet, database, graphics, and basic telecommunications software.

- Presentation and multimedia authoring tools (e.g., HyperStudio).

- Image editing software (e.g., Adobe Photoshop – often included with purchase of flat bed scanner.)

- Sound editing software.

- Search software capable of finding any targeted text in a wide variety of file formats. (This is especially important when you have downloaded large amounts of text from the Net.)

- Telecommunications software with a graphical user interface (e.g., Mosaic).

In addition to "shrink-wrapped" commercial titles, there are many excellent programs distributed as freeware (no fees) or shareware (free trial period and inexpensive purchase fee). These titles can be found in numerous online sources (e.g., America Online, etc.) or distributed on CD-ROM (e.g., Nautilus and Educorp CD-ROM's). While some of these programs are not very polished, some are excellent. This plan allows for the continuous active search for excellent software that meets our curricular and pedagogical objectives. While we recognize that shareware can be downloaded and tested for free, our software budget reflects the need to pay for any shareware titles that are used.

- What additional software titles or categories do you want to include? Remember that software decisions need to be driven by curricular and pedagogical objectives.

V. Staff Development

The goal of staff development is to provide opportunities for educators to acquire, refine and update their skills in areas of curriculum and pedagogy in ways that incorporate educational technology as a natural tool. While some technology-specific staff development is required, in general all technology-based instruction should be viewed in the larger context of the educational vision of the site.

Staff Development Focus Questions:

Professional Library
- Do you have a professional library for staff members with current subscriptions to educational journals, technology magazines, and other periodicals of interest to educators?

- Do you maintain a library of current books on educational practice, future societal trends, strategies for implementing change and other topics of interest to educators?

- Do you support "book reports" or "salons" in which educators spend time discussing books or articles they have read and applying what they have learned to their practice in the classroom?

Online Resources
- Does every educator have free access to online services from home, as well as from the site, that they can use to keep abreast of the latest issues confronting education?

- Does every educator know how to subscribe to the various newsgroups pertaining to education through which they can share ideas and ask questions?

- Has every NEA member taken advantage of the special reduced rates for America Online through which they can gain access to numerous educational resources as well as maintain dialogues with their peers?

- What technology do you have in place to allow educators to take part in statewide educational summits, "town hall" meetings and the like through the use of satellite downlinks?

Conferences
- How many *educational* (curricular and/or pedagogical) conferences per year does each educator attend through the sponsorship of the site?

- How many regional and/or national educational *technology* conferences per year does each educator attend through the sponsorship of the site?

- What budget for educational materials is each educator given to spend on educational materials discovered at the various conferences he/she attends?

Release Time
- How many days a year is each educator released to visit other classrooms at your site, or elsewhere, for the purpose of seeing or sharing exemplary practices with peers?

On-site Workshops
- How many days of staff development in pedagogy, curriculum, and technology is each educator granted each year with site sponsorship?

- How many days of follow-up to site-based staff development are provided for each day of workshop participation?

College and University Courses
- What plans are in place to alert educators to relevant courses offered at local colleges and universities to help them develop and maintain skills?

- What distance learning services are offered at the site (e.g., Tie-In, MEU, etc.)?

VI. Funding

The creation of a budget for your technology plan is essential, even if you don't have a ready source of funding identified. First, your funding section makes the plan real. Without it, the plan is just a brainstorming exercise. Second, if you already know how much you need to fund the plan, you'll be able to take immediate advantage of grant opportunities as they come up!

 Mariner

My recommendation is to create your funding plan in a spreadsheet (for example, using the Mariner shareware software on the CD-ROM) so you can make changes and additions and see the results immediately.

In developing a technology plan, funding has several components: capital expenses, and recurring costs. Given the rapid pace of technological development, it is probably most realistic to view all expenditures as recurring costs with different timelines. Some costs are incurred every year (e.g., telecommunications services, consumables, staff development, software and upgrades) while others may be renewed every five years or so (computers and other "capital" items).

In working out the funding portion of your plan, here are some ideas that might prove useful:

- Budget 30% or more of all technology expenditures for staff development. (Any less and you risk seeing the technology used not at all, or, worse yet, used to replicate an outdated curriculum.)

- Spend year-end money on software instead of hardware. New computers are often introduced during the summer break resulting in the arrival of outdated overpriced equipment in the Fall based on purchase orders cut during the previous school year. In the event that software is upgraded over the summer, most software vendors will provide free or very low-cost upgrade options in the Fall.

- Budget for ongoing consumable and maintenance expenditures.

- Think about your staffing needs. For example, if you are setting up a local BBS system for your sites, who is going to maintain it? Don't count on volunteer enthusiasm forever. (However, if appropriate, students might take over much of the responsibility as part of a class project.)

A Great Day for Shovelware

Where is the Life we have lost in living?
Where is the wisdom we have lost in knowledge?
Where is the knowledge we have lost in information?
— *T. S. Eliot, The Rock*

Where is the information we have lost in data?
— *George Gilder, Life After Television*

Introduction

One of my favorite fake advertisements broadcast on Saturday Night, Live! goes something like this: A tired teacher in a musty old classroom sits at his desk while students file by handing in their traditional "five-page reports" on some topic. The students look like disheveled leftovers from a Dickens novel, and their reports are handwritten in the largest handwriting they can get away with.

Finally, the last child approaches. Scrubbed clean, wearing a suit, he deposits, with great flair, a ponderous 300-page laser-printed tome replete with color pictures. As the teacher marvels at the crisp graphics that seem to leap from the page, this student looks at his classmates with a sneer of derision. The screen fades to black, and white text appears saying: "Macintosh: the power to crush the other kids."

Who among us would fail to be impressed by the sheer mass of this cleanly presented report, even before reading it! In fact, given its size, some would probably not even read the report in its entirety, and just give a high grade based largely on appearance alone.

This vignette came to mind during the period that the Shoemaker-Levy 9 comet was leaving Earth-sized pockmarks in the atmosphere of Jupiter.

This stellar light show started on Saturday, July 16, 1994. I imagined myself in the position of a teacher who, on Friday, assigned a report on this event, due on Tuesday, July 19. Given that some pieces of the comet hadn't hit the planet by the report's due date, the resources available to most students was (in my imagination) quite limited.

Well, let's look at two hypothetical student projects turned in on Tuesday. The first was submitted by a student who relied on traditional print resources for the report — newspaper articles, magazine articles, etc. This student didn't have much to choose from. Yes, there were a few articles appearing during the preceding months predicting the collision and speculating on what would happen when the comet completed its journey. The weekend papers had some coverage of the initial impact and a few photographs. Based on these limited materials, this student created a short report illustrated with a few pictures clipped from the newspaper, and spent a lot of time creating a well-thought-out report on this spectacular event.

Our second student had access to the Internet and, at the last possible moment on Monday evening, decided to start work on the report due the next morning. Using a program called Veronica to search databases on thousands of computers worldwide, this student found a treasure-trove of information on the comet impact, including an index of numerous full-color pictures available for downloading.

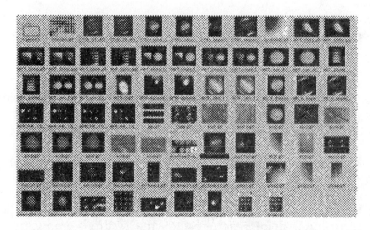

By selecting a large number of seemingly relevant text files, and a few dozen photographs, including those of the comet fragments strung out like pearls in space and some impressive collages of the various stages of impact plume development, this student was able, in about an hour, to create a 300-page double-spaced report based on the information accessible by scientists and students alike on the Internet.

Better Them Than Us: The Collision of Shoemaker-Levy 9 with Jupiter

A Report by
A. Student

Better Them Than Us, Part 1

One of the most spectacular events ever seen in our solar system is taking place this week as the pieces of a comet known as Shoemaker-Levy 9 are crashing into the atmosphere of Jupiter. Early pictures showing the plume caused by the impact are spectacular, as can be seen from this collage of images from the Calar Alto observatory.

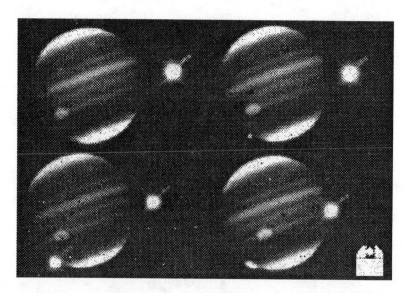

This impressive series of photographs (one of about 100 I have included in this report) shows the impact of the first fragment in the lower left edge of the planet over time. The bright spot to the right is one of Jupiter's moons, Io.

When the comet was observed, its train of 21 icy fragments stretched across 710 thousand miles (1.1 million km) of space, or 3 times the distance between Earth and the Moon. This required 6 WFPC exposures spaced along the comet train to include all the nuclei. The image was taken in red light.

The comet was approximately 410 million miles (660 million km) from Earth when the picture was taken, on a mid-July collision course with the gas giant planet Jupiter.

Credit: H.A. Weaver, T. E. Smith (Space Telescope Science Institute), and NASA

Image of Jupiter's cloud tops after the impact of the first fragment (A) of Comet Shoemaker-Levy 9 on 16 July. A violet (410 nm) filter of the Wide Field Camera 2 of the Hubble Space Telescope was used to make the image, which was taken at 5:32 EDT on 16 July 1994, 1.5 hours after the impact. The impact site is visible as a dark streak and crescent-shaped feature, several thousand kilometers in size, in the lower left of the image.

The comet entered the atmosphere from the south in the direction of the streak at an angle of about 45 degrees from the vertical. The crescent-shaped feature may be the remains of the plume that was ejected back along the entry path of the projectile. The features are probably dark particles from the comet, or possibly condensates dredged up from Jupiter's deep atmosphere. Comet Shoemaker-Levy 9 broke up during a close passage by Jupiter in July of 1992. The fragments will continue to impact the planet through 22 July 1994. Pre-encounter estimates of the energy of the impact are highly uncertain, and range up to that of a million hydrogen bombs (a million megatons of TNT).

Note: Text in this typeface is part of the hundreds and hundreds of pages of material the student downloaded from online resources!

137

Grading

Who would fail to be impressed with this display of scholarship? The report was beautifully printed on a color ink-jet printer, it was longer than the teacher's doctoral thesis, and it included the most up to the minute data available, including lots of things that hadn't made it into the daily paper.

If only one report was getting an "A" we might guess which one it would be — the one that looked the nicest, was the heaviest, and had material not found in the resources that were available on any newsstand.

In this case, that might be a tragic mistake.

It is quite possible that our Internet surfer downloaded information and shoveled it into a report without showing any understanding of the subject at all. Yet, given the size of the report, many teachers would be lured into providing a high grade without reading the document in depth, especially if 150 other high-school students had handed in their reports on the same day.

Rather than deserving an "A," our student might deserve a lower grade.

The ability to seek out and download information is very important. This student had to know how to use various online searching tools to locate all the information available on the comet collision. This information had to be transferred to the student's hard disk drive and had to be scanned for relevancy. These skills were also used by the student who went to the public library with two important differences: First, the traditional library search was largely carried out by hand, and, second, the traditional library had almost no in-depth information on the event being studied.

Our Internet surfer, on the other hand, quickly found that she was trying to get a drink of water from a fire hydrant. The deluge of information on this event was overwhelming, even in the early hours following the first impact. Rather than miss something important, our student simply downloaded everything available, especially photographs and their captions.

Properly arranged, these materials could be used to tell a coherent story. The skills of understanding and arranging these source materials should be rewarded (if done properly). This, after all, is what textbooks do, and we all know how lucrative THAT market is!

Beyond that, our student should be expected to make some creative contribution of her own — to draw her own conclusions from the information she so carefully (if quickly) gathered. It is her creative work that deserves the greatest reward. All the information used to support her conclusions is important, and can be included as an appendix, or even as extended quotations in her text. But in the absence of the organizational and creative elements, she has only demonstrated the (admittedly important) survival skill of all nomadic hunters and gatherers in cyberspace.

Synthesizing vs. Hunting and Gathering
What are we to do in a world where vast quantities of information can be downloaded by anyone with a modem and an account on a service provider?

Well, first, we need to overcome our natural desire to automatically favor reports just because they look nice. Yes, presentation is very important, but it is no replacement for scholarship.

Second, we need to insure that, even when all the reference material is included with the report, that every student expresses his or her own creative efforts.

Here's one suggestion:

Rather than give assignments with *minimum* page requirements (a holdover from the Information Age), Communication Age assignments might have a maximum page limitation instead.

Imagine what would have happened for our two students if the teacher had restricted the report length to one double-spaced page (with one-inch margins and a restriction to nothing less than 12-point type). Both students would have conducted the same research they did before, only now they both would have to show a capacity to synthesize what they had learned in a format that was tractable for all concerned (including the teacher).

The original 300-page download would be a great appendix to this report, but the distinction between the research and the student's original work would be quite easy to identify.

Grading could be broken into several components:

- Obtaining source material (1/3)
- Organization of this material into a coherent form (1/3)
- Synthesis, creation and support of an original idea based on this material (1/3)

(If the credit for information gathering seems high, remember that this assignment was given before the event to be studied had even occurred, and was due while the event was still in progress!)

How NOT to Respond

I've heard, on several occasions, from teachers who were furious with librarians who let students use on-line resources. They felt that students were somehow "cheating" if they didn't do their information search using only paper-based reference materials. One teacher asked, "How can we expect students to develop information research skills if they are allowed to use computers?"

Well that IS what computers are used for, right? Anyone who thinks that the paper-based world of reference materials is either complete or destined for a long life is seriously warped into the world of Ozzie and Harriet reruns. Even (and especially) scientific journals are moving on-line. It was scientists who first realized the power of the Net to share information with their colleagues. When our students log on, they gain access to the same databases as the professional scientific community — and they do so largely with that community's blessing!

No, the solution is not to restrict access to these databases. Instead, we need to encourage all students to gather information and then explain that information gathering alone reflects a tired old educational paradigm ill-suited to the needs of today's learners. We need to help students learn to organize and make sense of the voluminous quantity of information that streams across the Net every day.

If we don't, then every day will be a great day for shovelware.

Powertools for a New Era

If the only tool you have is a hammer, then every problem looks like a nail.

— *Abraham Maslow (attrib.)*

The grip of paper-based documents on education is quite strong. Paper has lots of advantages: It is cheap, "platform independent" (documents printed from Macs and MS-DOS computers can be read by the same people), it is transportable, and, unless you are reading by flashlight, you don't have to recharge your batteries every two hours.

On the other hand, paper has some limitations: Color is expensive, movies are hard to show (unless you flip the pages very quickly) and sound is virtually impossible to include with a report.

Certain types of documents should always be printed on paper, but student reports can often be better presented in other forms — interactive multimedia, for example.

The move to computer-based documents is not just a matter of paper not being "cyber enough" — it runs deeper than that.

JARGON ALERT - JARGON ALERT

The term "cyber enough" is modern parlance for "cool". It is often used by the PDB (people dressed in black) pretending to be multimedia mavens who live in or near San Francisco, drive the right cars, and show up at the right parties. These people often wear rimless glasses and an air of cool detachment from those who, clearly, aren't cyber enough. President Bush wasn't cyber at all. President Clinton is almost cyber. Vice-President Gore is cyber enough for most, but needs help now and then. People who are cyber enough actually take notes on $600 Newtons rather than 35¢ scratch pads. They read (or write for) such magazines as *Mondo 2000* and *WIRED* and have unlisted Internet addresses. The author of this document would be cyber enough if he had a Newton and more hair.

END OF JARGON ALERT - END OF JARGON ALERT

H'mmm, now, where was I? Oh, yes — multimedia reports.

The organizational and creative skills needed to create paper documents are wonderful, but they represent only one aspect of expressional skill. The beauty of multimedia authoring is that it allows students to pick the representational tool best fitted to the ideas being expressed. Text, color images, sounds, movies; all these and more can be combined into a single report that can be explored by anyone with access to a computer.

Using a multimedia authoring tool, students can create reports that can be read by one user, projected for the class to see using a color liquid crystal display plate, and archived as part of a portfolio documenting the achievements of each student.

The freedom to choose media elements appropriate for various parts of the report makes it easier for the student to clearly express his or her ideas.

Media are NOT interconvertible; a picture is NOT worth a thousand words. By making it as easy to incorporate color pictures as it is to create text, multimedia authoring by students provides them with the creative freedom they need to communicate their ideas to others.

Another compelling reason to support multimedia authoring by students is that it supports individual learning styles.

Howard Gardner's research on multiple intelligences (first reported in depth in his landmark book, *Frames of Mind*) shows that, in addition to our linguistic intelligence, we each have at least six others that (for some people) may be better vehicles for expressing ideas.

Some of us are visual and learn best from images. Others are more kinesthetic, and learn best when ideas are animated on the screen. The use of sound is critical to still others of us. Most importantly, each of us benefits when all our intelligences and sensory modalities are addressed. Paper can address one or two, but multimedia addresses them all .

Diogenes Revisited

Diogenes, you'll recall, was the Greek philosopher who used his lantern to search for an honest man. (His search was cut short when his lantern was stolen, but that's another story.)

Borrowing from the past, I went searching for multimedia creation tools suitable for use by all learners. To meet my criteria for excellence, these tools needed to be useful for everything from reports to presentations, and they needed to reek of quality.

They also needed to be free, or very inexpensive.

My search led me to a few titles included on the accompanying CD-ROM in the PowerTools folder. Some of the tools are free, some of them are "shareware" (in which case, PLEASE register and pay your shareware fee to the authors).

The tools we've included fall into several categories:

- Authoring/Presentation Software
- Image/Graphics Tools
- Sound Tools
- Other Neat Stuff

Authoring Tools

 DOCMaker

If there is one program on the CD-ROM that is a personal favorite, it is DOCMaker, written by Mark Wall (Shareware,

$25). This program started out as a way for people to include documentation with their software (hence its name). Historically, documentation files were text-based documents that could be read with tools like Apple's TeachText, or they were simple documents that could be opened with any word processor. DOCMaker provided another alternative: Documents that were self-contained applications. All you need in order to read a DOCMaker document is double-click on its icon.

Over the years, DOCMaker has added features without making the product difficult to use. When you first start the program, it looks like a text editor that supports multiple typefaces and sizes (but almost no document formatting). You are free to color your text if you wish, which is valuable of you are creating documents designed primarily to be read on a color display.

In addition to text, you can incorporate images into your documents and, in the latest version, turn any picture into a "button". This feature turns DOCMaker from a documentation tool into a multimedia authoring platform. When you create a document, you can choose to have a button click jump to another chapter, launch another application, print your document, quit the program, play a Macintosh sound resource, show a QuickTime movie, or bring up an annotation window.

We've included two chapters of this book in DOCMaker format on the enclosed CD-ROM. The first, based on the Goalposts chapter, illustrates the incorporation of annotated color images. (Just click on any image to see the annotations.) The second, based on the Technology Planning chapter, is just a plain text document ready for you to browse or print.

In addition to supporting the features mentioned above, DOCMaker documents can have many chapters and subchapters. You can build a hypertext table of contents that allows the reader to jump to any desired place with a mouse click or two. In addition, you can create documents that let the user conduct text searches for any words or phrases that might be in the chapter being viewed.

This program has a special place on my desktop. I like it so much that I use it to publish my Center's newsletter.

Quasi-relevant story

My introduction to this product came from viewing applications people had written in it. I was so impressed that I started calling computer stores to see if they had DOCMaker in stock. (I thought it was a traditional commercial product.) Finally, after getting a ton of "Never heard of it" responses, one software sales agent said, "Can you open a DOCMaker file right now?" I said I could, and opened one right away.

"Now," he said patiently, "move your mouse to the Apple menu and select the About This Document item."

I did and saw the shareware message and Mark Wall's e-mail address.

Oops.

 Museum

Museum is a delightfully simple application for creating presentations based on images, text and sounds. It has almost no barrier to entry. Mac users of ANY age can assemble a linear slideshow and save it for distribution to others. The version on the CD-ROM contains its own documentation as a default presentation. If you know how to cut and paste items from the scrapbook, you've got the skills to master this program.

GIF Slideshow

The idea behind this product is to let you peruse vast quantities of GIF images that you may have downloaded onto your computer system. Once you choose a folder, it is scanned for all the images that meet the correct format requirements, and a slideshow based on these images is started in alphabetical order. For a linear slideshow, you could create separate GIF files for each slide, name them slide 1, slide 2, etc., stick them in a folder and launch this program. This is a VERY easy program to master.

 PICTshow

This program is similar to GIF Slideshow, except that it displays other types of images as well (not JPEG, unfortunately) and has a few other features including spiffy transitions between slides. Try both and see which you prefer!

 JPEGView

This program is essential if you want to view your collection of JPEG images. JPEGView opens and displays images in many formats and lets you create a slideshow. What it lacks in transition effects it more than makes up for in its capacity to figure out what image format you are using. This program is so popular that major Internet programs like Mosaic expect you to be using it when displaying JPEG images.

Everybody Wants to be in Pictures

If you or your students are going to be creating multimedia documents, then graphics programs are important. Unless you are fairly talented, you'll probably be interested in using images you've collected from the Net, scanned in from your own photographs, or copied from CD-ROM-based image libraries whose pictures have been intentionally made available for your free use. In some cases, you'll be able to use these images just the way they are, and in others you'll want to modify them somewhat. Modifications can range from cropping or changing the size of an image all the way to serious image manipulation that makes the original image almost unrecognizable.

In any case, you need a program or two in your arsenal to create the final images you need.

Adobe's Photoshop is a terrific general purpose graphics program that will probably meet all your needs, but unless you got a copy bundled with your color scanner (a deal worth pursuing) you'll probably find its price tag a bit steep for classroom use. Fortunately, there are several public-domain and shareware graphics programs that will give you a lot of Photoshop's functionality for a fraction of the price.

Before describing the various graphics programs, I decided to show my face in unedited form. Using this as a starting image (and no, it didn't break the computer), I'll show modified copies after the description of each graphics program to illustrate the most bizarre effect I was able to create on short notice with each piece of software.

GraphicConverter

This program was mentioned in the Getting Wired chapter because of its ability to convert one image format to another. While this capability alone makes this software worth having, it only hints at the true power of the product. Images can be resized, resampled at different resolutions, edited, modified with a full set of paint tools, and transformed with a small set of "filters" that are similar to some of the effects in PhotoShop.

This effect was created with the Laplace filter. In color, the image has a blue-green background and the result is a bit Niemanesque.

While we are on the topic of graphics software, there are a few more programs you should know about.

 NIH Image

If you want more special effects (along with file conversion) then NIH Image is the program for you. This free program was created for the National Institute of Health for scientific image processing, but it also can be used to touch up that picture of Poopsie, the family mouse. The 87-page manual accompanying this program tells you more than you'll want to know, but is worth reading from cover to cover.

This picture resulted from use of the "emboss" filter in NIH image, making it look as if it were spray-painted on a stucco wall.

 Digital Camera

While we're on the topic of image manipulation, Digital Camera deserves a mention. In addition to providing some of the functionality of some of the other software listed above, this nifty program also lets you blend two images together for some truly spectacular special effects.

For example, I blended my picture with a picture of red bricks. Digital Camera let me choose how much of each picture to blend. I'm sure there is a practical application for this feature besides the intentional creation of double exposures.

 QuickGIF

QuickGIF lets you display GIF images and convert them to the standard Macintosh PICT format if you want. In addition, it provides a few special effects for transforming your image into a work of art.

I'm not sure why, but in addition to other effects, QuickGIF lets you transform your picture into an oil painting.

 PICTs to Movie

This handy tool has one task: to take a bunch of consecutively numbered PICT images and string them together into a QuickTime movie. Obviously, if all these images are wildly different from each other, the utility of this product would be less than obvious. But suppose that you have downloaded a series of satellite weather maps from the Net showing the cloud coverage in your area in one-hour increments. Using PICTs to Movie, these images can be turned into a movie showing the clouds moving across the country.

Here's how:

Step 1: Download a day's worth of satellite weather maps for your area from the Internet or a commercial service like America Online. These are likely to be GIF images larger than your computer's display screen.

Step 2: Use GraphicConverter to shrink the images to half-size and convert them to PICT format images. [Note: When you pay your shareware fee, you'll be able to just dump a folder-full of images onto the GraphicConverter icon and have it perform these tasks (or others that you want) automatically — another great reason for paying shareware fees!] The reason you want the images reduced in size is to insure smooth playback of the movie on your computer.

Step 3: Place the resulting PICT images in their own folder and rename them in chronological order (pict0, pict1, etc.)

Step 4: Start PICTs to Movie, choose your compression method (Cinepak takes a long time to compress, but produces the smoothest and nicest movies), and select the first picture in your sequence. (Follow the instructions given by the program.) Then, depending on the speed of your Mac, take a coffee break or go home, and the next thing you'll know, your collection of still images has been compressed into a truly wonderful movie!

I've included a couple of QuickTime movies made from collections of stills along with some sample satellite weather pictures for you to play with. They are in the Projects folder.

As an enterprising educator, you'll find all kinds of applications for this neat program!

Sounds Good to Me

While text and images have their place in multimedia documents, sound has an important role to play as well. Musical backgrounds can be composed and made part of your presentation, and royalty-free clip music libraries provide music and sound effects you can tailor for your project. In addition to these sounds, you or your students may want to provide some narration that is played as part of your presentation. In any case, you'll need to some software to record your sounds and save them in the format expected by your multimedia software. As with image editing, you have several choices. You can purchase a commercial product such as Sound Edit Pro, or you can use Sample Editor for free.

 Sample Editor

This is a remarkable program that has all but displaced the commercial sound edit programs on my hard drive.

Why?

Well, for starters, the user interface is quite pretty. You can easily record sounds of any length (limited by your computer's memory) and edit them to your heart's content. Clicks, pops, "um's" and other spoken glitches can be edited out to make your recording sound incredibly professional. In fact, the range of sound editing features offered in this program is so great that I'm hard-pressed to find a rationale for purchasing a commercial sound package unless I want to get into the CD recording business.

Sample Editor can save your sounds in either the AIFF for System Sound formats. If you need other formats, then all you need to do is use the SounsApp program to perform the conversion. Proper use of these two programs virtually guarantees that your recording can be created in a form compatible with any multimedia authoring tool you own.

Sample Editor comes with a very thorough user's manual, and supports some very nice features including fade in and fade out, level normalization, and, one of my favorites, cross fading. The cross fader works by mixing a sound in the clipboard with a selected portion of sound in the editor. The result starts out with the selected sound reducing in volume and the clipboard sound increasing in volume. While audio effects like this need to be used sparingly (see the manual for details), they have their place.

Searchin'

As I've said before, searching the Net is a lot like trying to get a drink of water from a fire hydrant. You'll be amazed at the sheer volume of text and pictures you'll be downloading. Let's say that you're interested in Jefferson's opinions on education (and I'm sure you are). Within a few minutes you'll be able to locate his treatise on the Commonwealth of Virginia on the Net and port a copy to your hard disk. (Actually, I've saved you the effort by putting it on the CD-ROM.)

Now what?

You could print it out and read it yourself (worth doing if you have the time) or you could use a special program to fish for any words in the document that might interest you. The problem is, what program do you use?

 Search Files

One program that gets a daily workout on my computers is called Search Files. It exists for one important task — to find any files containing text I'm searching for. I can select a disk drive holding many megabytes of documents, enter the word or phrase I'm looking for in the search field of this program, and wait a few seconds while everyone of these files is "read" by the program. As it is working, it builds a list of files containing the desired search word or phrase, and shows a portion of the sentence on each side of my selection so I can see the context in which the word appears. Once I've built a list of documents I want to explore more carefully, I can then open them with the appropriate software and select the passages I want to read in greater depth.

This handy program will search for text in all kinds of files, not just plain text documents. It will peer inside Hypercard stacks, word processor documents, and a host of other formats until it runs through every single file in the folder (or disk) I have selected for it to examine.

With the volume of information I scan every day, this program has probably kept me from going blind!

 ImageCatalog

While searching for a particular piece of text can be a painful experience, hunting for graphics is not that much better, especially if you've been downloading lots of pictures from the Net and you have no idea exactly what the picture name means. (This is especially true for space images downloaded from NASA.)

Commercial programs, can solve your problem by building catalogs of images for you. But why spend money when ImageCatalog will do the job for free? You can choose the size of the image as it will appear in the catalog (e.g., 120 x 100 pixels), and then drag all your images over the ImageCatalog icon and let it go to work building a catalog for you.

This program will recognize quite a few image formats — PICT, TIFF, GIF, JPEG, to name a few. The resulting catalog shows a reduced version of each image along with its name. Double-clicking on the catalog image opens the full-size image for you to see in detail (assuming ImageCatalog can find the original image). You can print the catalog, or save it to your hard disk for browsing when you want to find that picture you know you downloaded, but have no idea what it is called.

EasyPlay

If your goal is to catalog (and play) QuickTime movies, then the EasyPlay shareware program will fit your needs wonderfully. In addition to allowing you to play QuickTime movies, this program will build catalogs of your film clips in a catalog containing a "poster" image (usually the first frame of the film) along with the title of the clip, and its location on your hard drive. You can also edit the entry to include any other information you wish to incorporate in the catalog. In addition to cataloging movies, this program will catalog PICT images as well.

POTS and PANS: Kitchen Table Reflections on the Future

All information looks like noise until you break the code.

Neal Stephenson

I've saved the last chapter of this book as a place for more open-ended speculations on the impact of the Communication Age on education. This chapter's title refers to POTS refers to ("Plain Old Telephone Service") and PANS ("Pretty Amazing New Stuff"). The subtitle comes from one of my favorite places for thinking (and writing): a sunlit kitchen table in my Monterey, California office. There's something about the proximity to the ocean, the sound of barking sea lions and the overall ambiance of this magical place that makes it good for thinking.

The Intersection of Information and Geography

In William Gibson's book, *Virtual Light*, he refers to bike messengers as working at the intersection of information and geography. This vision, created by the originator of the word "cyberspace", started a flood of thoughts, some of which I would like to share with you.

Consider the world of researchers in the Information Age. Armed with the tools of their trade, they can still be seen in the great libraries and museums of the world studying collections firsthand in support of their work. I, myself, was prepared some years ago to embark on a journey to trace ancient footsteps from Fez, Morocco to the Alhambra in Granada, Spain, documenting the intricate geometrical tiling patterns that so enchanted M. C. Escher that they ended up making his name synonymous with artwork based on tessellated figures. This journey many thousands of miles from my home was clearly a quest in search of the intersection of information and geography.

While I never made that trip, I speculated on a similar journey in *Education, Technology, and Paradigms of Change for the 21st Century*, as a result of a sabbatical spent in the great museums and cathedrals of Europe. What would it be like, I wondered, if students were freed from the geographical strapping tape binding them to their school buildings? What is a school if not a community of learners; and, wherever communities of learners exist, is that place not a school?

Bob Albrecht, a pioneer promoting personal computing before personal computers were invented, used to argue vehemently that children could learn far more if left to roam free through San Francisco's Exploratorium than they could in most classrooms. The Exploratorium's hands-on approach to learning stood in stark contrast to most other museums and classrooms with their static collection of ossified information frozen for eternity in the form of lifeless artifacts. The Exploratorium is a protean learning place — an intersection between information and geography.

And now, at the dawn of the Communication Age, a new vision beckons — virtuality. If we cannot *physically* visit the great museums, libraries, rain forests and other geographically scattered sacred sites of learning, why can't we go there *psychically*, through the medium of virtual reality?

This vision of a parallel universe constructed from nothing but bits lies at the crossroads of science fiction and reality — so much so that not much is to be gained by distinguishing between the two. In Neal Stephenson's *Snowcrash* we are exposed to the Metaverse — a parallel virtual world not unlike the World Wide Web, but with better graphics. The only thing keeping Stephenson's world from being built out of today's

MUDs (Multi-User Domains) is that bandwidth is not yet cheap enough (although it soon will be).

In our rush to construct such worlds, we need to keep track of what is being lost, and what is being gained. Virtual worlds have their place, but they will never replace the physical worlds they try to emulate — they serve a different purpose and they operate under different constraints.

I remember standing in the Museé d'Orsay a mere foot from one of Vincent van Gogh's self portraits. I'd seen reproductions of this painting many times, and had even acquired a disk-based copy somewhere. But here I was, face to face with the product of one of the artistic geniuses of all time.

And as I stood there, so close I could reach out and touch the picture, I realized that I was crying.

Virtual Museums

Museums serve a unique role in the education of the public. The popularity of museums is so great that when, for example, the Monterey Bay Aquarium opened its doors over a decade ago, lines of visitors stretched far down the block waiting to enter. Even now this institution, and many others, are deluged with visitors curious to learn more about the subjects represented by the museum's area of focus.

Unlike traditional classrooms in which material is presented at a pace and sequence determined by a teacher, many museums offer a more casual experience. Exhibits can be explored in any sequence the visitors desire. Some will spend a lot of time focused on one particular exhibit, and others will opt for a whirlwind tour of the entire place. Museums typically host people with a wide range of skills and interests. For this reason, most exhibits need to be comprehensible to those for whom the subject is fairly new. This makes museums ideal places for people to have their interest sparked in a subject area that they might wish to pursue in depth later.

While this "random-access" aspect of museums is one of their great strengths, it also generates one of a museum's great challenges: how to address the needs of those who wish to explore the topic of an exhibit in more depth.

Consider the case of a visitor to the Monterey Bay Aquarium from a small town in the Midwest. This visitor might be entranced (as many are) by the aquarium's display of jellyfish, and wish to learn more about these incredible creatures. Like many museums, the Monterey Aquarium has a book and gift shop featuring titles and artifacts thematically related to the exhibits. It also has a research department, and a staff of well-trained docents who are on the floor to answer questions.

Our hypothetical visitor might learn a bit from the docents, but their time is spread among the thousands of visitors in the building at any given time. The book store has a nice collection of titles on marine life, and our visitor might find a title or two to be of interest. Access to the research staff is generally harder to secure, especially since these dedicated people are often focused on the design of new exhibits, or on ongoing research in their areas of specialty. In short, the options to learn more about jellyfish are limited, even at the aquarium.

The challenge is compounded when our visitor returns home to a land-locked community many hundreds of miles away from the nearest jellyfish. Suppose that the decision to learn more about this topic is made long after the return home. What then? Depending on community resources, our visitor might find some help from the local library. If he or she is close to a college or university that grants public access to its libraries, the odds of getting more information are improved, but our incipient marine biologist might live in an area remote from the informational resources taken for granted by residents of larger cities. In this case, he/she may decide that the task just isn't worth it, and give up.

Museum bookstores serve a tremendous role but they are limited in their capacity to meet the needs of those who want to continue their new-found interest in a topic. First, their shelf space is limited, and they naturally wish to cater to as large an audience as possible, since their sales help support the institution that houses them. This means they are not likely to carry materials that are too deep for general audiences to comprehend. Second, books on science-related topics are often painfully out of date by the time they are published. While their general perspectives might be accurate, the details might be severely flawed when viewed in the light of recent discoveries in the field.

Instead of visitors having to rely just on books in stores and libraries, imagine that anyone visiting the museum could return electronically anytime he or she wished, from anywhere in the world. And what if this return visit not only allows displays to be viewed again, but also lets the visitor could move "behind" the display to explore its content in any level of depth desired? Then suppose that this same visitor could collect in-depth reference material and pose focused questions to experts in the field for clarification — anywhere these experts might be on the planet. And then, for fast-moving fields of study, why not have the reference material provide a historical context for the subject, and offer access to up-to-the-minute information as soon as it is disseminated.

Such a virtual museum would meet the needs of novice and expert alike. It would provide a forum for discourse among experts, as well as for discovery by neophytes. It would be open to everyone, any time, any place, 24-hours a day, 365 days a year — all from the privacy of one's home, place of work, or study.

The virtual museum I've just described is possible today through the medium of telecomputing, and will become one of the prime artifacts of the Communication Age.

How it works

Let's say that our visitor to the aquarium expresses an interest in one of the exhibits, and wishes to learn more. The docent or store clerk would then offer our friend a computer disk (for sale at a nominal fee) that could be used on his/her home computer. At any later date, the visitor could insert this disk, boot up the main program and, through the computer's modem, be automatically connected to the museum's computer system which might not be at the museum — in fact, it might be a network of computers spread throughout the world!

Once the visitor connected to the system (an automatic process), he/she would be presented with a graphical image of the museum site that could be navigated with a mouse. Once in a desired location, exhibits in that area could be brought onto the screen for examination. If more information were desired, on-screen options would provide access to in-depth explorations, references to other exhibits, lists of resources, etc. Before leaving an area to visit another one, the program user might be asked if he/she has any questions to ask of experts in the field. If so, the question would be forwarded to the relevant expert whose answer would be made available the next time he/she logs on.

This virtual museum is in no way meant to replace an actual visit. Ideally it supports actual visits becuase, no matter how powerful telecomputing technology is likely to become in the next few years, it will always lack the sensory richness of an actual visit.

Pragmatic Realities of Today's POTS
Today's home-based computer systems communicate over standard "plain old telephone service" (POTS). This limits data transmission rates to anywhere from a few hundred characters per second to about a thousand characters per second, depending on the speed and quality of the modem used. Even at the higher end of this scale, the transmission of graphical data is time consuming. For this reason, the bulk of the graphics (e.g., the museum layout and snapshots of individual exhibits) will be preprogrammed on the original disk. If exhibits are removed or changed, then, when the user logs on, the image library on the user's disk can be updated before the session begins.

A Sample Tour of Tomorrow's PANS

In the world of "pretty amazing new stuff" (PANS) an ideal virtual visit allows the participant to leap through ideas at his or her own pace, following the thread of an idea, and leaving a trail that can be followed or backtracked later. Imagine a tour of the Virtual White House. Mouse clicks take the participant from room to room, and into close proximity with the incredible works of art on display. A painting catches our visitor's fancy. Up close, she finds it is a work by Gilbert Stuart and notes that some of his other works are displayed on the Mall at the National Gallery of Art. Grabbing a copy of the painting in the White House, she "leaps" to the National Gallery, directly to the painting of her choice. She can temporarily hang the picture from the White House next to the painting in the National Gallery for side-by side comparison.

She becomes so lost in thought that she is startled to find others beside her in the gallery choosing to look at both paintings themselves. Using her keyboard or voice (her choice) she can talk with the others present. These gallery visitors may or may not look like they do in the "real world". That would be their choice. They might (and probably would be) physically located in diverse spots all over the planet. Yet, for a while at least, they share a virtual space where they can converse with others who share their interests.

After browsing some more, our visitor creates a collection of her favorite pictures and associated text files to transfer to her computer's hard disk.

In some ways this visit is richer than an actual one (curators frown when visitors move paintings from one place to another). In other cases it is poorer — she can't have lunch with her new-found friends, although they can exchange enough information to let them get together if they are in the same city. The non-technical challenge in creating such virtual museums is to design them in ways that make effective use of the new medium. Ideally, symbiosis is created when the virtual and physical worlds blend in this way. The result is greater than the sum of its parts.

How long will we have to wait for highly-graphical virtual museums? Text-based worlds of the kind I've described already exist. They are called MUD's or MOO's ("multi-user domains" and "MUD object oriented"). Several visually-oriented worlds are being designed now, and I expect the first of these to open for televisitors within a year.

Video Conferencing

Two-way video conferencing tools like CU-SeeMe are important not for what they do, but for what they portend.

I was returning to California from a presentation in Kentucky and changed planes in Dallas. On my way to the connecting flight, I saw a huge Intel exhibit staffed by people demonstrating ProShare — their video conferencing and document sharing system. (By the way, how about a few points for ecumenicism in this otherwise Mac-biased book!) I chatted and looked at the moving image of a participant in Oregon who had me fill out a form on the Dallas airport-based computer that was immediately available to him over the ISDN line connecting us.

I'm sure the significance of this event was lost on the airlines, just as the railroads never thought about those passengers taking their trains to see the new airplanes. ("Let's boost business by sponsoring rail trips to air shows!")

Here, in the lion's den, Communication Age technology was a demonstrable driving force for the permanent loss of business travel — and the airlines didn't even notice.

It is amazing the pains to which we'll go to move atoms when we could be moving bits.

I was on my way home from a one-hour keynote address. I'd spent most of one day getting to my destination, and was about halfway through the lengthy trip back — ten hours in airplanes and ten hours in a hotel room, all in support of a one-hour talk. This kind of business travel is commonplace as people zip from coast to coast to attend short meetings that could be held (complete with two-way video) electronically.

And here, in the Dallas airport, thousands of business travelers were being shown an alternative to physical travel that, for the price of one or two business trips, would free them from the joys of sitting in an aluminum tube breathing recycled air and eating peanuts from a plastic pouch that requires a hunting knife to open.

There are merits to travel — peripheral vision is poor in cyberspace, and the friendships that emerge from casual conversations are less likely to happen when encounters are limited to talking heads bouncing in freeze-dried vignettes on a small window on your computer screen. But, as I have said, bandwidth is becoming free, and that means the images will improve. As they do, more and more people will make the shift to videoconferencing and cross-country jaunts for a one-hour business meeting will be seen as anachronistic holdovers from a culture powered by petroleum, rather than by bits in cyberspace.

Will all business travel disappear? Of course not. Many important aspects of human communication just don't make it across the infosphere. But for all those that do, the airlines are vulnerable.

What do these new technologies mean for education? Do they mark the end of the human touch? I think not. In fact, they make it all the more important as we craft learning communities for the next century.

Campfires in Cyberspace

The existence of learning communities probably predates civilization. As we embark on our great adventure into the infosphere, we can see path markers in the primordial dirt roads of consciousness.

A key aspect of archetypal learning environments can be found in a tale I first heard from Gregory Bateson:

165

One day, someone sitting at a computer keyboard entered the following question: "Do you suppose that computers will someday think like humans?" After processing this request for some time, the computer displayed the following response: "That reminds me of a story...."

Embedded in this tale of Bateson's is an important observation: One of the distinguishing features of humans is that we are storytellers. In fact, with the possible exception of certain marine mammals, we may be the only storytelling species in existence.

The Campfire

For thousands of years, storytelling was a mechanism for teaching. While it was not the only mechanism, it was (and is) an important one. Through storytelling, the wisdom of elders was passed to the next generation. Good stories have always embodied a blend of the cognitive and affective domains — in fact, in story, there is no separation between the two. For example, one version of a creation story told among the indigenous peoples of the American Northwest has Raven bringing light to the planet after it had been hidden away by Grandfather. He had hidden the light because he wanted to believe that his daughter was the most beautiful creature in the Universe, and could only hold that belief if he never saw her. Through trickery, Raven steals the light and, through mishap, creates the sun and the stars. This one story embodies not only the cosmological aspects of the people's belief, but also the metaphorical aspect of "being kept in the dark".

This quality of nuance and multiple interpretations is common to storytelling. It is one reason that adults and children can enjoy the same story together — each age takes appropriate elements from the story. The power of storytelling is so great that even in more recent times (c. 250 BC,) we find Socrates responding to his students on occasion with the Greek equivalent of "That reminds me of a story."

There is a sacred quality to teaching as storytelling, and this activity took place in sacred places, typically around the fire. The focal point of the flame, the sounds of the night, all provide backdrop to the storyteller who shares wisdom with students who, in their turn, become storytellers to the next generation. In this manner, culture replicates itself through the DNA of myth. The often tangential nature of storytelling, its use of metaphor, its indirect attack on a topic, all combine to make storytelling an effective way to address topics that might be too confrontational to address head on. Story crafts its own helix around a topic. As Robert Frost said, "We sit in the circle and suppose, while the truth sits in the center and knows."

And so, from an archetypal perspective, the campfire represents an important aspect of the learning community. It does not, however, stand alone.

The Watering Hole
Just as campfires resonate deeply across space and time, watering holes have an equal status in the pantheon of learning places. Virtually every hominid on the planet has, at one time in its historical existence, needed to gather at a central source for water. During these trips to the watering hole, people shared information with their neighbors — those within their own village, as well as those from neighboring villages and travelers on their way to or from a distant village. The watering hole became a place where we learned from our peers — where we shared the news of the day. This informal setting for learning provided a different kind of learning community from that of the shaman or troubadour who regaled us from the podium of the campfire. The learning at the watering hole was less formal. It was peer teaching, a sharing of the rumors, news, gossip, dreams and discoveries that drive us forward. Each participant at the watering hole is both learner and teacher at the same time.

Just as water is necessary for survival, the informational aspect of the watering hole is essential for cultural survival. I'll have more to say about this later. For now, suffice it to say that the watering hole is alive and well in corporations where people gather around the water cooler (or, more recently, the copying machine) to continue a tradition of archetypal proportions. Executives and support personnel alike reenact on a daily basis scenes that have been played out on the plains of Africa for tens of thousands of years. Any disconnection from this informal learning community risks a disconnection from one of the things that makes us human.

The Cave

The learning community of the campfire brings us in contact with experts, and that of the watering hole connects us to our peers. There is one other primordial learning environment of great importance: the cave — where we come in contact with ourselves.

Through legends and artifacts we know that, throughout the planet, learners have needed, on occasion, to isolate themselves from others in order to gain special insights. Whether these periods of isolation took place in the forest, or in caves, whether they were the subject of great ritual, or just casual encounters with personal insight, the importance of having time alone with one's thoughts has been known for millennia.

The "vision quest" practiced by some indigenous peoples of the Americas represents one of the more formalized renditions of this practice. After a lengthy period of preparation, the learner is led to a cave with nothing but a blanket and is left for two days without food. During this time, through meditation, the learner may have a vision that can shape or guide him or her through the next phase of life. In addition of being a place of learning, the vision quest also becomes a rite of passage.

This rite of passage has another interpretation in modern parlance: the passage of knowledge from an externally accepted to an internally held belief. This internal "knowing" involves far more than memorization — it involves true insight. When Carl Jung was asked in his later years if he believed in God, he smiled and said, "I don't believe, I know."

We all have times in learning any subject when we need to internalize that knowledge. For Newton, it may have been under an apple tree. For Moses, it was the wilderness. For us, this internalization may take place during a walk in the woods, but is just as likely to take place during a quiet moment (or day, or week) in relative seclusion in a library (another sacred place), office, bedroom, kitchen or den.

Learners have long gathered around campfires, watering holes, and have isolated themselves in the seclusion of caves. They have experienced all these learning environments in balance and, if the balance was offset, learning suffered.

A Modern Example
In my line of work, I spend a great amount of time attending professional conferences. These gatherings bring together experts who share their insights with large audiences over a period of two or three days. Over the course of the conference, one can see examples of all three learning metaphors in action.

For example, every December, there is a mathematics conference held at the Asilomar conference center near Monterey, California. A thousand or so school teachers gather for a weekend at the beautiful location on the Pacific coast to learn more about the teaching of mathematics. Numerous presenters share their insights through formal, scheduled presentations. Exhibitors have their wares on display in a separate hall. Meals are held in a huge dining room, and lodging is on-site so people with common interests can share their ideas into the early hours of the morning.

A visitor to this conference would see, at any given time, examples of all three learning environments. Some attendees sit in conference rooms listening to experts sharing their insights. The glow of the campfire is replaced by that of the projection screen, but the metaphor of the shaman or troubadour remains intact.

Outside these conference rooms, other participants gather at the exhibit hall, shuttle bus stops, main lodge, or other gathering places where they will be sharing ideas with each other. These interactions range from choosing an off-campus restaurant for a special dinner, to sharing new strategies for introducing calculus to children in middle school. In the absence of a clearly defined watering hole, gathering spots are chosen by convenience. As in the film, *Field of Dreams*, "if you build it, they will come." The exhibit hall, Asilomar lodge and dining hall are probably the closest this conference comes to providing metaphorical watering holes.

In addition to the two settings in which people are grouped together, the conference visitor would also see people walking by themselves along the trails through the dunes to the ocean shore. Individuals might sit for hours looking at the water, exploring the trees on the grounds, or otherwise engaging in quiet thought. This "cave time" is facilitated by the nature of the Asilomar site. In fact, the ability of this one site to support all three of these learning environments probably accounts for its great popularity as a conference center, even if these multiple aspects of the facility are never overtly addressed.

It is interesting to note, by the way, that conference programs almost never mention anything other than the "campfire" aspects of the conference. Participants are invited to attend conferences to "hear the latest from experts in the field". While this has great merit, this aspect of a learning community represents only one third of the food for thought in a balanced meal for the mind.

In sharp contrast, I had the opportunity some time ago to see what happens when a conference is out of balance. A major invitational conference of educational technology in Washington, D. C. had brought an audience of about 600 highly regarded experts together for an intensive two days of presentations. The presentations were set up back to back, with no breaks until lunch, and then again after lunch with no breaks until dinner.

The presentations were (generally) excellent. For example, Arthur C. Clarke held us spellbound with his visions of the future during a live two-way remote videoconference from Sri Lanka. Even so, by lunch on the first day, many attendees were grumbling. They had been exposed to some intense campfires with no access to watering holes or caves. The conference was so tightly scheduled that several people complained of "overload". On the one hand, people were free to walk out of sessions they didn't like, but the presentations were of such high caliber (or the presenters so well known) that most people were reluctant to walk out. Even so, by the second day, the audience started to build in breaks where none existed.

This experience brought home to me the importance of scheduling opportunities for the three types of learning experiences, and showed the importance of maintaining balance among all three.

While I've concentrated on the application of these archetypal learning models to conferences, they apply to classroom settings as well. Students have experienced the campfire of the traditional classroom setting and relied on the playground for their watering hole. Quiet time for reflection, when made available, takes place in libraries or study halls, or is deferred until the student goes home at the end of the day. The watering hole is being brought into classrooms today through the medium of cooperative learning but, tragically, school libraries (and the time to spend in them) are "at-risk" in schools where funding for such programs is in short supply.

Campfires in the Communication Age
Now that we've entered the Communication Age , we have the opportunity to explore how these primordial metaphors for learning map into the telecosm. First, and make no mistake here, all three sacred learning spaces will have analogs in cyberspace. If they don't, then cyberspace will cease to exist as a domain of interaction among humans. Those using the new media will create their own analogs for these learning places, even if they are not designed into the system. In this regard, cyberspace is like any other frontier: rich in possibility,

covered with brambles and weeds, but with fertile soil ready for development.

At first blush, it appears that the world of multimedia computing most closely resembles the domain of the campfire (at least as currently practiced). The educational software market is replete with CD-ROM-based programs that turn the computer display screen into a colorful animated canvas on which ideas take shape and through which information is presented. The integration of text, sounds, color images and animated sequences provide many of the same tools for engagement known to the ancient storytellers, even if their images were conjured primarily through the mind's eye.

If it is the case that the glow of the campfire has been replaced by that of the computer monitor, we must ask if the stories being flickering from the modern fire are as compelling as those told around the old one. At this time, it is generous to say that the field is still sorting itself out. Multimedia is a new medium and quality products will not exist until the authors and publishers understand that mere transcriptions from the world of print or linear video does not automatically produce good educational software. McLuhan tried to tell us this. It is time to listen! We must realize that the world of interactive multimedia is completely different from anything we have worked with before.

For example, in the world of oral tradition and the printed page, stories have two aspects. They have a beginning, middle and end, and they have conflict and resolution. In this Aristotelian world of storytelling, the conflict and resolution are the figure played against the ground of beginning, middle and end. We have certain expectations for such stories. They start with "Once upon a time...," and they end with some variation of "happily ever after". In the meantime, we are presented with a situation involving some conflict that, in general, gets resolved by the time the story ends. This model probably predates recorded history and is ubiquitous.

While new media can be used to tell stories in this fashion, the power of interactivity lets us move beyond the linear presentation of material. One possibility is to invert the Aristotelian world by creating a conflict to be resolved (the ground) and then to allow the user, through interaction with the multimedia software, to resolve the conflict through the creation of a unique story with its own beginning middle and end. This figure/ground reversal is possible because new media are not frozen in time. Unlike static words and images created by a storyteller, the learner can craft dynamic resolutions to a challenge created by a new breed of storymaker.

The Myth of Interactivity

It can be argued that virtually all multimedia products on the market today do provide some measure of interactivity. While this is true, the interactivity in some products is so limited that the flexibility I want for users is nonexistent. For example, many pieces of "interactive" storytelling software merely allow the user to choose the pace at which a linear story unfolds. True interactivity provides, at the minimum, the capacity to branch to different scenarios, to gather additional information, to take new twists and turns and, when very well done, to explore avenues never anticipated by the creator of the program.

Viewed in the context of the figure/ground reversal mentioned above, the weakness of many current multimedia titles can be seen: When users are just clicking buttons to progress through a linear story told by another, multimedia becomes nothing more than high-tech page turning. On the other hand, when the user can craft a personal pathway through the content, even if the material is already in place, this freedom of true interactivity supports the creation of unique ways to resolve the conflict established at the start of the story. Interactivity of this type is rewarding at many levels. It facilitates creativity and the development of thinking skills by the participant in the journey through storyspace.

All of this is possible with the multimedia tools available today. The major limitation comes from the mindsets of those who craft products — otherwise well-intentioned people who, in many cases, are concerned with keeping development costs to a minimum, and with getting products out the door in a hurry. The craft of multimedia design is not a linear mix of writing, image creation, sound composition, and selective placement of "button clicks" to advance to the next page. It is, instead, the storytellers' craft writ large — a new medium of expression whose ideas cannot be captured or presented in any other medium.

We are experiencing the birth pains of this new craft, and it promises to be a noisy baby.

Watering Holes in Cyberspace

If interactive multimedia represents at least one facet of campfires in cyberspace, then telecommunications represents a vast global watering hole. These services are distributed throughout the world, and are connect to each other and to individual users through a complex web of networks, both public and private.

Users of telecomputing services send messages to each other (e-mail) and take part in real-time conferences with other users. This peer-to-peer dialog resembles the traditional watering hole activity with several special differences. First, rather than limiting discourse to people in a fixed geographic area, this watering hole is planetary in scope. Information and geography no longer intersect.

Second, today's limitations of telecomputing restrict most interactions to text-based messages. This provides some measure of anonymity to the users of the system. A message in pure text form conveys no information about gender, age, disability, appearance — such an environment provides the opportunity to work with thoughts in themselves, devoid of other interpretations and biases that we might apply inadvertently if we engaged in face-to-face meetings.

174

This blessing is, unfortunately, also telecomputing's curse. When we have a peer-to-peer chat on any subject we wish, this interaction lacks the richness of face-to-face meetings. It is fine for topics of the intellect, but limited for affairs of the heart. One cannot shake hands, smile, or hug through the medium of telecomputing — yet.

Cybercaves

Many of the same telecomputing services that provide electronic watering holes also provide vast resources of information that can be searched, extracted, added to, and commented upon by anyone with the interest to pursue them. As I've shown in previous chapters, anyone can log onto NASA computers to download the latest images from space, or access Library of Congress archives, university libraries, government agencies, and even some private corporations. The Internet is so complex that navigating through it bears some similarities to listening to short-wave radio — there is some wonderful stuff out there, but it takes patience and diligence to find it.

The information-providing aspect of these services sets the stage for electronic caves — places where pursuers of knowledge can gather information in their quest for understanding or discovery. Working in isolation, threads of an idea can be pursued through the movement of fingers over a keyboard, rather than by running up and down library aisles extracting references from printed documents. Once the raw information is gathered and downloaded to the user's computer, he or she can then work in privacy to examine, interconnect and otherwise draw meaning from the results of the search.

While telecomputing services provide one form of electronic cave, libraries of information, images, sounds, movies, and programs — all stored on CD-ROM's — provide another. Each CD-ROM, a plastic disc the same size as those dominating the music industry today, can hold the equivalent of 275,000 pages of single-spaced text — information that in printed form would require the sacrifice of 23 trees just to provide the paper.

One of the greatest merits of the electronic cave, whether it is accessed through phone lines or through laser beams hitting a plastic disc, is that information of interest can be found with automated searching methods that free the user to concentrate on the underlying quest without being encumbered by the magnitude or dynamics of the searching process. This capability stands in stark contrast to information published in paper form. For example, short of reading an entire document to isolate a particular piece of information, most of us depend on the document's index to narrow our search. However, many documents lack an index; and those that do have one may not have entries for the topics of interest to us, or, if they do, may list those entries under key words other than those we might choose.

In the electronic world, once a document is loaded into a computer, the occurrence of any word can be pinpointed in a fraction of a second. This power of electronic searching allows us to keep our quest foremost in mind — it lets us explore conceptual space at the speed of thought.

H. B. Gelatt correctly states: "While information is food for thought, it isn't the whole meal." By simplifying the process for locating information, our computers facilitate the harvesting of background information from which we synthesize and extend our own discoveries in our quest for knowledge and wisdom.

Telecosmic Nightmares — When Nothing Works
The power of computer-based multimedia and telecommunications can be harnessed to provide modern analogs to our primordial tools of learning. Left to our own devices, many productive users of technology have gravitated to their own best mix of these applications. The challenge that faces us comes from institutionalized attempts to see technology as a replacement for one aspect of these modes of learning without thinking about the need for balance.

For example, let's examine distance learning as it is most commonly practiced.

On several occasions I've had the opportunity to conduct courses for educators through "distance learning". I was located in a television studio, and students were located in cities all over the country where they could see and hear me through satellite transmission from my site. The return path from students was an 800-number they could call to respond to me by voice. Students could not talk with their peers at other locations (although they could, of course, talk with peers located at the same site). The studio in which I was located typically had two cameras — one framing my head and shoulders, and another hanging above a drawing pad on which I could place printed "overheads" or draw on paper with a pen. My movements and gestures were hampered, and spontaneity was difficult because I couldn't see my audience. Furthermore, voice contact lacked spontaneity because of the time delay associated with shipping my signal through a geostationary satellite located some 24,000 miles above us.

Since my style is highly interactive, I found this environment to be quite stifling. On the other hand, I've encountered some educators who just love it. From their perspective, it doesn't matter if they see their students or not. They are content to be the talking head dispensing information to an invisible audience. As far as they are concerned, their role is not to engage in human discourse, it is simply to present information and hope it is received. This is a weak attempt to create a campfire because the embers are all but extinguished by the fountain-of-wisdom educator. As for watering holes and caves — they have no place in this type of distance learning world.

While existing distance learning environments of the type I've described may be helpful to those for whom other options are not possible, I see them as mere high-tech replicas of an outdated classroom model.

Telecosmic Dreams

In the world of slow telecommunications, the multimedia campfire was far removed from the telecommunity's watering hole. Now that cheap bandwidth is increasing by leaps and bounds, and the price of high-speed access to the Net is dropping, these two worlds are starting to merge.

One has to be careful when bringing water to fire. If splashed on the flames, water can extinguish the fire; but, if heated in a pot, the water can be transformed into steam. The transformation of water into steam provides the greatest promise for education.

The revolution brought on by the Communication Age can transform education in exciting ways. How will we use the power of this new medium? The choice is up to us. And, whatever choice we make, we will do well to remember Jean Houston's observation that myth is the DNA of the human psyche, and that education is a uniquely human craft.

Postscript: Waiting for Baudot

I've based this book on the emergence of the Communication Age — an era marked by incredible advances in perceived bandwidth that will change how we live, work and play.

Like all revolutions, this one will touch some people more readily than others. One of the major concerns being expressed today is how to avoid creating a bifurcated world populated by information "haves" and "have-nots". I am convinced that, in time, the advances of the Communication Age will reach everyone. I am also aware that, for the next year or so, some people (and many schools) will be restricted to information transfer using ordinary voice grade phone lines. Does this mean that those people will be bypassed by the Communication Age, that their computers risk becoming silicon armadillos abandoned at the side of the information highway?

The answer, fortunately, is "no". Everyone will be able to explore this new world, even if we have to use creativity in place of bandwidth.

Digital data speeds are measured in "baud", a unit of measure named in honor of the 19th century inventor and communications pioneer, J. M. E. Baudot. One baud is roughly (but not exactly) the same as one bit per second. When I first started using networks to send information to a computer, I used a terminal that operated at 110 baud — roughly ten characters per second. I still remember how powerful I felt when I moved to a 300 baud (30 character per second) modem in the early 1970's. From there I moved to 1200 baud, then to 2400 baud, and today I feel anxious if I have to use anything slower than a 9600 baud modem.

It never ceases to amaze me how the modem we were thrilled to use one day becomes unacceptable as soon as we move to the next higher speed. We are all speed demons in this regard, looking for the next burst of speed to expand our capabilities on the Net.

High bandwidth pipelines capable of carrying vast amounts of multimedia information are the hallmark of the Communication Age. These services exist today — for a price — just as computers existed in the 1960's for those with the resources to afford them. And, just as incredibly powerful computers can be purchased today for a fraction of the price paid for yesterday's relics, high-bandwidth communication lines will, someday, be incredibly cheap. For example, Intel has announced a TV cable modem that will be available for about $300 in 1995 and will allow cybernauts to receive information at a speed of 30 million bits/sec. By mid-1994, similar devices were already being used in test-markets at speeds of 6 million bits/sec.

For those who are happily sending short e-mail messages and text files at 1200-2400 baud, the idea of transporting billions of bits per second is a mildly interesting notion belonging to a fantasy world of the future. For those who are ready to take advantage of Communication Age tools like multimedia teleconferencing, that future can't come soon enough.

The problem comes when we run up against the limitations of the telephone lines in our homes, offices, or classrooms that were designed for the transmission of voice alone — and we (for whatever reason) just can't get high-speed digital lines installed.

Products like ProShare for the Windows platform and ShareVision or CU-SeeMe for the Macintosh provide two-way video and voice links along with the ability to share screens of information, provided users have access to ISDN lines, or other high-bandwidth pipelines. Users can chat with each other, see each other's moving images, and work on documents jointly.

They can do this because the fast data communication path (typically 112,000 bits/second or higher), combined with splendid data compression tools, allows vast quantities of information to change hands in close to "real time" — a speed approaching that of a live face-to-face meeting.

Can you achieve a similar result on your regular phone lines? As it turns out, you can.

The solution to this problem is not to send all the information in "real time", but to send libraries of common data to everyone taking part in a "virtual conference" ahead of time. Once everyone has the same data libraries on their computers, the only information that needs to be sent are commands that trigger the display of a previously loaded document, or information on the position of a cursor as it sketches pictures on an electronic whiteboard. By sending data that triggers events in the recipient's computer, rather than sending the information itself, incredible efficiencies result.

 The Virtual Meeting

One product that operates this way is The Virtual Meeting by RTZ Software. A demo version of this software is included on the CD-ROM, so you can try it yourself.

This product lets you connect with colleagues at remote sites using any combination of local area networks, telephone lines, or other communication pathways at your disposal. To take full advantage of the product, you need two connections — one for voice, and one for data. The voice connection is just your plain old telephone, probably hooked up as a speakerphone for hands-free operation. The data connection can be a second phone line hooked to a modem at each end, or it can consist of any local or wide area network at your disposal.

Here's how it works. Let's say a student wants to present a multimedia report to colleagues at another school. She would first assemble all the media elements (slideshows, pictures,

QuickTime videos, etc.) and then send these to the other site by mail, or through the network. These files would then be loaded in the computers at both ends of the line along with scanned pictures of the participants (if desired). At the appointed time, our student would call her colleagues at the remote site and ask them to launch The Virtual Meeting software. She would then start her own copy of the program and establish a connection. Once that happens, any presentation she opens on her computer will be opened on the remote computer as well. Her mouse clicks are echoed to the other system to insure that the remote site sees the same things she does.

If even more interactivity is desired, she can open an electronic whiteboard that can be used by any participant to sketch pictures that everyone else sees. She can transfer control of the presentation to the remote site, add other sites, and generally have the freedom that would come from a live presentation with everyone in the same room.

She cannot (over ordinary phone lines) send moving pictures of herself. She can, however, have her picture appear on the remote screen if it was included with the files that were distributed to all remote sites. And, if the remote users sent their pictures to her, those images would appear anytime they were interacting with the program.

Because this software doesn't have to send the actual data, it can operate over ordinary phone lines with a slow speed modem! The key to this ability is that The Virtual Meeting only sends "Apple events" — keystrokes and mouse clicks, not huge picture files.

When I first saw this program, I experienced an incredible case of déjà vu. Many years ago, in the late 1970's, I co-developed a similar system with Roy Lahr when he and I were both connected with the Xerox Palo Alto Research Center. We never did anything with the technology, and I am delighted that someone finally has!

Do products like this mean that we shouldn't bother with high-speed connections? Not in the least. There are many things we can do with high-bandwidth connections that are incredibly cumbersome or virtually impossible to do otherwise.

At the same time, products like The Virtual Meeting show that no one needs to be left behind as we move into the Communication Age. There is plenty for us to do while waiting for Baudot.

Glossary of Terms

Every craft has its jargon, and the world of computers and communication is no exception. The following brief glossary defines a few of the terms you are likely to encounter in your ongoing adventures into cyberspace.

Baud: The speed at which modems transfer data. One baud is roughly equal to one bit per second. It takes eight bits to make up one letter or character. Modems rarely transfer data at exactly the same speed as their listed baud rate because of static or computer problems. More expensive modems use systems, such as Microcom Network Protocol (MNP), which can correct for these errors or which "compress"data to speed up transmission.

Cyberspace: A word coined by William Gibson in his sci-fi classic, *Neuromancer*, to describe the Net. Today the word is commonly used to describe the universe of electronic information represented by all the interconnected networks, and computers scattered all over the world. Once you start exploring the Net yourself, you will probably notice that it has a feeling of "placeness" to it.

Download: Copy a file from a host system to your computer. There are several different methods, or protocols, for downloading files, most of which periodically check the file as it is being copied to ensure no information is inadvertently destroyed or damaged during the process. Some, such as XMODEM, only let you download one file at a time. Others, such as batch-YMODEM and ZMODEM, let you type in the names of several files at once, which are then automatically downloaded.

E-mail: Electronic mail — a way to send a private message to somebody else on the Net. Used as both noun and verb.

FAQ: Frequently Asked Questions. A compilation of answers to these. Many Usenet newsgroups have these files, which are posted once a month or so for beginners.

Freeware: Software that doesn't cost anything.

FTP: File-transfer Protocol. A system for transferring files across the Net. Sometimes this term is used as a verb: "To get this picture, just ftp to photo.si.edu." Anonymous ftp sites are available for public access file retrieval, although sometimes access is restricted to certain times of the day.

Gopher: A menu-driven navigational tool for finding resources on the Internet.

Host system: A public-access site; provides Net access to people outside the research and government community.

Internet: A worldwide system for linking smaller computer networks together. Networks connected through the Internet use a particular set of communications standards to communicate, known as TCP/IP.

Listserv: A tool for distributing messages to a list of subscribers who have a shared interest in some subject. Once a message is sent to the list server, copies are immediately sent to everyone on the list.

Log on/log in: Connect to a host system or public-access site.

Log off: Disconnect from a host system.

Lurk: To browse a subscribed newsgroup without posting anything.

Mailing list: Essentially a conference in which messages are delivered right to your mailbox, instead of to a Usenet newsgroup. You get on these by sending a message to a specific e-mail address, which is often that of a computer that automates the process.

Mosaic: A program for the creation of interactive multimedia documents in which the various pictures, movies, sounds, and other resources are located in various remote sites on the Net.

Net: Another way of referring to the Internet (today) or the NII (soon).

Network: A communications system that links two or more computers. It can be as simple as a cable strung between two computers a few feet apart or as complex as hundreds of thousands of computers around the world linked through fiber optic cables, phone lines and satellites.

Newsgroup: A Usenet conference.

Online: When your computer is connected to an online service, bulletin-board system or public-access site.

Post: To compose a message for a Usenet newsgroup and then send it out for others to see.

Server: A computer that can distribute information or files automatically in response to specifically worded e-mail requests.

Shareware: Software that is freely available on the Net, but which, if you like and use it, you should send in the fee requested by the author, whose name and address will be found in a file distributed with the software.

Snail mail: Mail that comes through a slot in your front door.

Telnet: A program that lets you connect to other computers on the Internet.

Usenet newsgroup: A repository of "news" items ranging from messages to pictures, sounds, movies, and computer software. Subscribers are notified when new material germane to their interest is posted. They then access the items from the newsgroup itself. Unlike listservs, newsgroups are stored in a central location rather than sent to every subscriber as e-mail.

Veronica: A program that searches Gopher servers based on keywords provided by the user.

Bibliography

Howard Gardner, *Frames of Mind*, Basic Books, 1983.

William Gibson, *Virtual Light*, Seal Books, 1993.

George Gilder, *Life After Television (Revised Edition)*, Norton, 1994.

Ira Magaziner, et al., *America's Choice: High Skills or Low Wages*, National Center on Education and the Economy, 1990.

Lynn Martin, et al., *What Work Requires of Schools: A SCANS Report for America 2000*, U. S. Dept. of Labor, 1991.

Robert Reich, *The Work of Nations: Preparing Ourselves for 21st Century Capitalism*, Vintage Books, 1992.

Neal Stephenson, *Snow Crash*, Bantam Books, 1993.

David Thornburg, *Education, Technology, and Paradigms of Change for the 21st Century*, Starsong, 1991.

David Thornburg, *Edutrends 2010: Restructuring, Technology, and the Future of Education*, Starsong, 1992.

Alvin Toffler, *The Third Wave*, William Morrow and Company, 1980.